But I Say Unto You,...

D1452898

JOHN G. REISINGER

Crowne Publications, Inc.
P.O. Box 688
Southbridge, Massachusetts 01550

Printed in the United States of America.

ISBN 0-925703-04-4

Acknowledgements

To the many pastors and friends who kept encouraging me to put into print the things in this book. It was these people who helped me think through the issues involved in understanding the sovereign grace of God.

To Dr. Robert A. Morey, for editorial skills and constructive criticism.

Table of Contents

ONE

The Full And Final Authority of Jesus Christ

Y ou have heard that it was said, "Do not commit adultery." **BUT I TELL YOU** that anyone who looks at a women lustfully has already committed adultery with her in his heart.

> Matthew 5:27,28

You have heard that it was said, "Eye for eye, and tooth for tooth." **BUT I TELL YOU**, Do not resist an evil person. If someone strikes you on the right cheek, turn to him the other also.

> Matthew 5:38,39

You have heard that it was said, "Love your neighbor and hate your enemies." **BUT I TELL YOU:** love your enemies and pray for those who persecute you.

> Matthew 5:43,44

It has been said, "Anyone who divorces his wife must give her a certificate of divorce." **BUT I TELL YOU** that anyone who divorces his wife, except for marital unfaithfulness, causes her to become an adulteress, and anyone who marries the divorced woman commits adultery.

> Matthew 5:31,32 NIV

How are we to understand Christ's teaching in the Sermon

1

on the Mount as it relates to our present relationship to the Law of Moses? Is Christ contrasting His teaching with the Law of Moses in the above verses? Or, is He only contradicting the Pharisee's interpretation of Mosaic Law?

Are we, as Christians, to urge our government to write into the law of the land today the "eye for eye and tooth for tooth" system of justice given to Israel? Can such a system be reconciled with the "turn the other cheek" words of Christ in the Sermon on the Mount? Is Christ really setting up a "new system" of controlling personal behavior, or is that a false conclusion reached by not understanding what He really meant?

The answers to these questions involve identifying the person, or persons, with whom Christ is contrasting Himself when He says "but I say unto you," and then understanding the foundation of the radical difference set forth in the contrast? It is obvious that Christ is making some kind of contrast between His teaching and former Jewish teachers. Is Moses himself one of those "teachers of old time" or is Christ contrasting Himself only with the wrong interpretation of Moses by the older Rabbinical leaders? In other words, is the entire thrust of the Sermon on the Mount merely Christ giving us the true and spiritual meaning of what Moses really meant, or is Christ also contrasting His teaching and authority with the laws and authority of Moses?

Is Christ giving the Church a new canon of moral conduct based entirely on grace as the foundation of His kingdom or is He merely reaffirming the Law of Moses? Is Christ establishing a totally new kingdom based on grace and giving a new and higher canon of moral conduct, or is both the foundation and canon of moral conduct of Christ's kingdom the same as that of theocratic Israel?

Perhaps the real question must somehow involve the relationship between "law and grace." Is Christ saying exactly the same thing that Paul said in Romans 6:14 " . . . *you are not under the law but under grace?*" Is Christ actually contrasting the rules one must apply in personal behavior under a covenant of law as opposed to the rules one applies when living under a covenant of grace? Or, is there really no contrast at all in the Sermon on the Mount between "law and grace"? Are both Israel and the Church under different *administrations* of the same *covenant* and therefore under the same moral canon of conduct, or did

Christ establish a New Covenant that demands much higher and more spiritual conduct from His people?

All of the foregoing questions are involved in the correct understanding of the Sermon on the Mount. How we answer these questions will usually be dictated to us by the particular theological system that we have adopted. Our purpose in this book is to set forth how we arrived at the following three conclusions:

One: The Sermon on the Mount is an integral part of the Christian's rule of life today and not the rules for a future kingdom, therefore I disagree with the "dispensational" view as it is expressed in the first edition of the *Scofield Reference Bible*.

Two: Christ never contradicts Moses in the sense that Moses was in any way wrong. We believe in the unity of the Scriptures. Christ does, however, give the Church new and higher standards, or rules of conduct, than Moses ever gave, or could have given, under a covenant of law, but this in no way means or implies that Moses was wrong. It means that Christ is literally a new and superior Lawgiver than Moses because He administers a new and *"better covenant based on better promises. . . . "* (Heb. 8:6). It means that grace can make higher demands than law can make simply because of the nature and power of grace. Grace cannot only appeal to a higher motive and make higher demands, it can also *empower the fulfillment of those demands.*

Three: Under a system of covenant law, we cannot legislate and punish the thoughts of the heart. God has both the right and power to condemn a person for immoral day dreaming in his tent, but neither Moses nor the law covenant that he gave could have someone stoned to death for wicked thoughts. It is clear that Israel was punished by God for the sin of covetousness (Isa. 57:17; Jer. 6:13-15); However, this was a direct sovereign act of the God Who sees into the heart and not punishment at the hands of a magistrate administering the law. Under the New Covenant, the Holy Spirit is the personal pedagogue of every believer and He can deal with the heart in a way that the magistrate could not under the Old Covenant given through Moses.

It seems quite evident that Christ is actually saying far more in the Sermon on the Mount than just "This is what Moses **really** meant." Christ is saying, "I am in no way destroying or criticizing Moses. I am applying his commandments in an area and in a manner that neither he nor his law covenant could ever have done. I am also giving My disciples new laws that make moral and spiritual demands that are based entirely on grace instead of the Old Covenant of law." In establishing these points we will avoid the two extremes that lead to serious and opposite errors. On the one hand, we will protect the true "unity of the Scriptures" and not have Christ contradicting Moses, and on the other hand, we will not limit the authority of Christ by making Him to be a mere "rubber stamp" of Moses. We will allow Christ to give new and higher truth that Moses never gave.

We will see that Christ is clearly contrasting the legal rule of Moses (which was "holy, righteous, and good") with His own gracious rule (which is higher, gracious, and better) in such a way that demonstrates the truth that Christ is indeed "**THAT PROPHET**" (Dt. 18:15; John 1:21; Acts 3:26) Who would replace and supersede Moses as the new and final Lawgiver over the Church. The New Covenant established by Christ is a new and better *covenant* with new and higher laws and not just a new *administration* of an older covenant and the same laws.

Here is a summary of what will be set forth in this study of some of the "But I say unto you" contrasts in **Mt. 5-7:**

Christ never says or implies that anything in the Old Testament Scriptures was wrong in and of itself. Remember that the God of Moses Who spoke the Law at Sinai is the same God Who spoke His grace at Calvary in our Lord Jesus Christ. John says, *"The Law was given by Moses, but grace and truth came by Jesus Christ"* (John 1:17), but in both cases it was the same God speaking and working toward the same goal even if the rule of law and the rule of grace contain different canons of conduct during a given period.

However, in our zeal to be sure that Christ does not contradict Moses, we cannot have Christ merely "rubber stamping" Moses as an equal teacher of God's truth. Any system of theology that leaves Moses as "the big man on Campus" in the conscience of a believer today has not heard "My beloved Son" speaking clearly. The "but I say unto you" contrasts in the Sermon on the Mount can have some new truth that Moses never gave without demeaning Moses in any way. I fear some well meaning people have lost the unique and final authority of Christ as Lord and Lawgiver of the Church in their zeal to protect their view of the "unity of the covenants" and also their particular view of the "perpetuity of the moral (Old Covenant) law."

We must see that Moses is *finished*. He has been replaced with Someone greater and better. The covenant of Moses was done away simply because it was obsolete (Heb. 8:6-13). Moses did his job and he did it most faithfully. Both he and the covenant he administered were good and glorious (Rom 7:12; II Cor 3:7-11). Moses was faithful in God's house (Heb. 4:2,5) as the *pedagogue* (Gal. 3:24), but his ministry or service in the house is finished. A greater than Moses is here and He has built the new and true house of God that was promised to David (I Chron. 17:12). Our Lord, the *Son* **IN** Whom God has fully spoken **FINAL** truth (Heb. 1:1-3), has replaced Moses, the *servant* **THROUGH** whom God spoke **PARTIAL** and **PREPARATORY** truth. Christ supersedes and replaces Moses as the true and final Lawgiver in the same way that He supersedes and replaces Aaron as the true and final High Priest.

Christ does not contradict Moses any more than He contradicts Aaron even though He replaced both of them and their ministries. Both Aaron and Moses were faithful and Godly men but neither of their ministries could "cleanse the conscience" (Heb. 9:14,15; 10:1-4) and effect the goal of redemption because of the "weaknesses" involved in the Old Covenant arrangement (Heb. 8:6-13). Both Aaron and Moses, along with their respective ministries and the legal covenant upon which those ministries were founded, had to be replaced by our Lord Jesus Christ and the New Covenant that He established. *Moses could no more give a complete and full canon of moral conduct before the advent of the Holy Spirit on the Day of Pentecost than Aaron could offer a final and complete sacrifice for sin before the death of Christ on the final Day of Atonement!*

Christ replaced Moses in the same manner that Paul and the other apostles replaced John the Baptist and the other Old Testament prophets. In fact, Paul, by inspiration of the Holy Spirit Whom Christ had promised to send (John 16:12-15), adds to the earthly ministry of Christ Himself (I Cor. 7:10-12) by giving more truth. Paul is not contradicting Christ when he adds new laws to cover a situation that could not have existed before the formal establishing of the Church of Christ. The Holy Spirit was given for the express purpose of revealing truth that Christ could not give because the disciples were unable to grasp it at that time.

Should we take the words of Christ in John 16:13 literally? Or
does "guide you into all truth" only mean that the Holy Spirit
would "rightly interpret what Moses really meant?"

Paul is not destroying Christ when he adds another ground
for divorce besides adultery to the teaching of Christ? Paul's
authority for writing, and the new laws that he wrote, did not
in any way come as "logical deductions" from either the Law
of Moses or from the words of Christ in the Gospels. It was *new
revelation*. Paul gave the Church a distinctly new rule concerning divorce that added to what Christ had taught, and, in so doing, Paul was claiming that Apostolic authority was all he needed
to literally "add to the Word of God" and change the rules of
divorce even further than Christ had changed the laws that Moses
had given. Must we strangle progressive revelation in order to
hold on to a wrong view of the "unchanging moral law of God?"

It is essential that we see that Christ never contradicted Moses.
And it is also essential that we see that Christ *did indeed replace*
Moses. Christ sometimes takes the same moral laws that Moses
ministered as a Law Covenant and raises them to a higher level
than Moses ever could. The same laws take on a new and unique
character when the Hands that bring them have holes in them
instead of a sword. Under the New Covenant, Christ also gives
new laws of behavior based on grace that Moses could never have
given under a covenant of law. When we say "Christ gives new
laws," we are assuming that everyone believes that the inspired
words of the Apostles are equally the words of the risen and en-
throned Christ.

TWO

★ ★ ★

Various Views of the Sermon On the Mount

Perhaps it might be well to list the major approaches to understanding the Sermon on the Mount before we look at the passage. It might help some people that are having problems with their presently held system of theology to realize there are other options besides Dispensationalism and Covenant Theology.

1. The **SOCIAL GOSPEL** view: Jesus is teaching us how to live so we can "earn the mercy and grace of God and become Christians." The beatitudes are set forth as the way to earn salvation. This is salvation by works and a contradiction of the gospel of salvation by grace. This view totally denies the cross and the need of a blood sacrifice to cleanse guilty sinners. We reject it as a total denial of the Gospel.

2. The **LIBERAL** view: Jesus is contrasting the true "Christian view of a loving God" with the "tribal concept of the Old Testament God of vengeance." The "eye for an eye" type of law is "sub-human" and not worthy of any enlightened person. It is pure paganism. This view deliberately rejects the authority and inspiration of both the Old and New Testament Scriptures. Any view that pits the Old Testament against the New Testament in a way that even suggests that the same God is not moving toward the same goal in both cases has not understood either testament. This view does more than deny the Gospel. It consciously attacks and seeks to destroy the Gospel.

7

3. The **HISTORIC DISPENSATIONAL** *view:*[1] This view states that the Sermon on the Mount is not given to the Church but is purely Jewish. It is the "Law of the Kingdom" (millennial reign of Christ in the future). The laws in the Sermon on the Mount are the "legal" rules for the future kingdom age, or millennium. The Jews rejected this earthly kingdom when Christ offered it to them and it was "postponed" until after the Second Coming of Christ. At that time all of these "legal" laws will be in force. However, until that time we must never apply "kingdom truth" to the Church today. A Christian may draw some beautiful and helpful "applications" from the Sermon on the Mount since all of Scripture is written **TO** us even though all of it is not **FOR** us. The Epistles of Paul, which first make known the doctrine of the Church, are the believer's rule of life during the Church age. The following quotation from the *Scofield Reference Bible* is typical of this view:

> Having announced the kingdom of heaven as "at hand," the King, in Mt. 5-7, declares the principles of the Kingdom. The Sermon on the Mount has a twofold application: (1) Literally to the kingdom. In this sense it gives the divine constitution for the righteous government of the earth. Whenever the kingdom of heaven is established on earth it will be according to that constitution . . . the Sermon on the Mount in its primary application gives **neither the privilege nor the duty of the Church. These are found in the epistles**[2]. . . . (2) But there is a *beautiful   moral   application   to   the Christian*. . . . These principles fundamentally reappear in the teaching of the Epistles.[3]

As stated earlier, we reject this approach to the Sermon on the Mount. This view creates a tension between law (Israel) and grace (Church) in God's eternal purposes that makes it impossible to see the Church as the true "Israel of God" to whom the covenant promises to Abraham were really made.

4. The view of **Classical Covenant Theology:**[4] This view agrees that the Sermon on the Mount contains the "rules of the kingdom," but insists that the kingdom is here and now and not in the future. Covenant Theology insists that Christ was not in any way contrasting Himself, His teaching, or His authority with

Moses. He was only contradicting the wrong interpretations and additions to Moses. Christ was merely giving us the true spiritual meaning of Moses as contrasted with the Rabbinical distortions.

We agree that this view is partially true, but it is not nearly all of the truth. It simply does not go far enough. It never touches the heart of the issue. Like Dispensationalism, this view interprets the new in light of the old and cannot allow many statements in the New Testament Scriptures, especially those passages that contrast law and grace, to be taken literally. This view confuses the unity of the *covenants* with the true unity of the *Scriptures*. Martyn Lloyd-Jones, in the following quotation, has given an accurate criticism of this view although at times he seems to accept this view himself:

> Another view, which is perhaps a little more serious for us, is that which regards the Sermon on the Mount as nothing but an **elaboration or an exposition of the mosaic law.** Our Lord, it is maintained, realized that the Pharisees and Scribes and other teachers of the people were **misrepresenting the law,** as given by God to the people through Moses; what He does, therefore, in the Sermon on the Mount is to elaborate and **expound the mosaic law,** giving it a higher spiritual content. This is a more serious view, obviously; and I feel it is **totally inadequate** if for no other reason than that it, also, fails to take account of the Beatitudes. The Beatitudes immediately take us into a realm that is **beyond the law of Moses** completely. The Sermon on the Mount **does expound and explain the law** at certain points—but it **goes beyond it.** [5]

The one thing concerning the Sermon on the Mount about which Covenant Theology is adamant is that Christ may never in any way contrast Himself with Moses. Christ may *interpret* Moses but He dare not *add anything new* to Moses. In no sense whatever can Christ be a "new Lawgiver" in Covenant Theology. At most He may give the true spiritual teaching of the law, but He cannot either add to it or raise it to a higher level with new demands. We wholeheartedly endorse what Lloyd-Jones said concerning this view. Christ was indeed showing the spirituality of the law as opposed to the Pharisees' carnalizing the law, but, as Lloyd-Jones said, Christ also "goes beyond" the Law of Moses and adds new and higher laws.

The Dispensational view insists that the Sermon on the Mount is all Jewish and is not for this present age. Covenant Theology teaches that absolutely nothing in the Sermon on the Mount (or the rest of the New Testament Scriptures) is really *new in the area of ethics and morals.* According to Covenant Theology, Jesus was not giving either new or more spiritual rules for conduct simply because the *highest possible spiritual rules* had already been given once and for all time at Mount Sinai on the Tablets of Stone. The Law of Moses, correctly understood, is just as *spiritual* as anything that Christ ever taught! No teaching in any New Testament passage will ever be higher spiritually or more important to our understanding of holiness and moral duty than a correct interpretation of the "Ten Words" written on stone.

A.W. Pink is representative of this view:

> Christ is **not** here [Mt. 5:28-42] pitting Himself against the Mosaic law, nor is He inculcating a **superior spirituality.** Instead He continues the same course as He had followed in the context, namely to define that righteousness demanded of His followers, which was more excellent than the one taught and practiced by the Scribes and Pharisees; and this He does by exposing their error and expounding the **spirituality of the moral law.**
>
> . . . our Lord's design in these verses has been misapprehended, the prevailing but erroneous idea being held that they set forth the vastly **superior moral standard of the New Covenant** over that which was obtained under Judaism. . . . [6]

Pink is forced to make the above statements simply because his view does not see Christ as a true *new Lawgiver* but only as a "rubber stamp" of Moses. Under the guise of protecting Moses and the "moral law," this view demeans Christ and misses the higher moral law of Christ. Covenant Theology insists that when Christ and His Apostles talk about a *New Covenant* (I Cor. 11:25; Heb. 8:6-13) they don't mean there actually is a literal *New Covenant* with any new or different laws; they really mean a *new administration* of the *same* covenant and same moral laws that Israel was already under. This is why Covenant Theology can claim that the Old Covenant written on the tablets of stone is higher and more important than *even the Sermon on the Mount.* Here is a typical example, from R.L. Dabney, of what we mean:

> The whole Decalogue is found written out in full in two places in the Bible. . . . It is the **doctrine of the Catechism**[7] that these "Ten Words" were intended to be a summary of man's whole duty. Why, it may be asked, is **so much made of them**? Why not make **equal account** of some verses taken from Proverbs, **or the Sermon on the Mount?**[8]

Dabney frankly admits that the Law of Moses is more important to him than Christ's Sermon on the Mount. Dabney may not have intended his exaltation of Moses to minimize both the authority of Christ and the New Testament epistles. However, this is exactly what his statement does. Once you accept the idea that the Ten Commandments are the highest moral law ever given, it must effect your attitude to the authority of the New Testament Scriptures in the area of ethics and morals.

Dabney's view, clearly expressed in the statement quoted above, produces a mentality of "two tier" ethics and the Decalogue will always be the highest tier. The Tablets of Stone are "God's unchanging *law*," and the rest of the Scripture, including the Sermon on the Mount, is subservient to this rock of granite. God's laws will always carry more weight in the conscience of a believer than the mere *"Scriptural advice"* in the Epistle of Paul. Paul's *"admonitions"* to husbands and wives in Ephesians is good Scriptural *advice* that we are urged to obey in order to have a happy marriage. However, the **LAW** of God is a different matter altogether. We dare not, under pain of death, break any of God's *commandments*. It is impossible to treat Paul's imperative commandments as having equal authority with the Law of Moses as long as our mind and conscience are controlled by Covenant Theology's system of two tier ethics.

We repeat, Dabney may not have intended to blunt the force and effectiveness of the New Testament Epistles in the Christian's conscience. But that is the sure result whenever the Ten Commandments are exalted above the rest of the Bible and looked upon as **God's** unchanging **Law** and the Book of Ephesians is **Paul's** inspired **directives**. The Ten Commandments cannot be viewed as the *highest* moral standard in the Bible without every-thing else, including the Sermon on the Mount, becoming lesser. In Dabney's view, neither Christ nor any of His Apostles can change or in any way add to the ethics and morality of the "highest standard" already written in Tables of Stone.

It is a fact beyond dispute that in both preaching and prac-tice there are "the *commandments* of God" (the Tables of Stone) and the "*exhortations* of Paul," and we all know which ones are the greatest and most important. Sinai is the highest mountain in all of Scripture according to Covenant Theology. Such a view cannot escape the mentality of "mortal sins" (breaking God's law) and "venial sins" (failing to practice one of the **principles** given by the Apostle Paul).

It seems to us that Dispensationalism cannot let Moses *INTO the New Testament* in any sense, and Covenant Theology can-not get Moses *OUT OF the New Testament* in any sense. One sys-tem has Christ contradicting Moses and the other system has Christ merely "rubber stamping" Moses. Perhaps both systems are half right and half wrong. Maybe both have some truth and we, by taking an either/or approach, are losing a part of God's truth.

When I first entertained the above possibility in my mind, I decided to make sure that I avoided both of the major errors us-ually connected with studying the relationship of the Old and New Testaments. I put a stake on the left hand side and said, "If Christ ever contradicts Moses in the sense that Moses was *wrong*, then I have gone past this stake and I am denying the basic unity of the Scriptures."[9] I put another stake down on the right side and said, "If I wind up making Christ nothing but *co-equal with Moses* as a teacher of God's truth, or worse, if I subordinate Christ to Moses as Dabney does, then I am going past this stake and I am denying the supremacy of the Lord Jesus Christ and the New Testament Scriptures." I was sure that Christ never contradicted Moses, but I also knew that our Lord was more than on an equal par with Moses. It was at that time that I reached the conclusions that led me to the position that is set forth in this book.

5. The PROMISE/FULFILLMENT, or New Covenant, view. This view starts with the New Testament Scriptures and allows them to mean exactly what they say. Christ is seen as asserting His unique and final authority as the New Lawgiver by giving a new

and higher canon of conduct to the Church. He is most assuredly correcting the perversions of the Pharisees, but He is also clearly giving new and higher truth that Moses never taught. Christ sometimes applies the same truth that Moses taught but does so in a manner that Moses could never have done. At other times Christ is making new and more spiritual demands on His disciples because of their being "under grace." Neither Moses nor the law covenant could ever have made these demands or laws.

This fifth view sees both truth and error in Dispensationalism and Covenant Theology. It is based on an understanding of the nature and relationship of the two major covenants (the Old legal Covenant with Israel at Sinai and the New gracious Covenant that replaces it) in Scripture (Jer. 31:33; Heb. 8:6-13; Gal. 4:21-31). This view sees Christ establishing a distinctly New Covenant in His blood and inaugurating a new age with the giving of the Holy Spirit at Pentecost. However, it also insists that this present "new age" in which we now live is the inauguration of the kingdom promised in the Old Testament Scriptures. We now live in the "times of the Messiah" envisioned by the Old Testament prophets.

It is now time to examine the Scriptures themselves and see if we can prove our statements. We will look carefully at the four texts in the Sermon on the Mount quoted at the beginning of chapter one and see exactly what Christ meant when He said "But I say unto you." We will consider the methods used to explain each of the four texts, and see that in all four cases the usual explanations will be only partially true. They will not cover all of the truth nor will they usually get to the heart of the issue. In some instances the explanations are essential to the maintaining of a specific theological system even though the arguments used often contradict other passages of Scripture.

---

[1]I used the word "Historic" deliberately. When I use the word "Dispensational" in this paper, I am referring to the system as set forth in the first edition of the *Scofield Reference Bible* and taught by *Dallas Theological Seminary*. I am aware that many people today will call themselves "Dispensational" who will reject some of the things taught by either, or both, of these sources. I use these two sources only as clear points of references so as to avoid either caricature or misunderstanding. Each person must decide where he fits today. I think everyone will acknowledge that the above two sources give an accurate and clear view of Dispensationalism as understood and believed historically. Some men have recently modified their views to such a degree that it is questionable

whether they have the right to apply the term "Dispensational" to themselves.

[2]When words are written in either **bold** or all CAPITALS inside of a quotation from another author, it means that **I** am emphasizing something that the writer did not emphasize.

[3]*Scofield Reference Bible*, first edition, p. 1000.

[4]When I use the term "Covenant Theology" in this paper, I am referring to the system of theology set forth in the *Westminster Confession of Faith* and taught at Westminster Theological Seminary. I use these two sources only as reference points. I am sure that everyone will agree that these two sources represent Covenant Theology as it has been understood historically. As with Dispensationalism, some men today are modifying their views to the extent that the basic foundation of the system is being denied. However, there has been no attempt whatever to change the *Westminster Confession of Faith* as the accepted standard nor has its "authority" been questioned by those who subscribe to it.

[5]D. Martyn Lloyd-Jones, *Studies in the Sermon on the Mount*, Wm. B. Eerdmans Pub Co, p 14.

[6]A.W. Pink, *An Exposition of the Sermon on the Mount*, Bible Truth Depot, p 110, 127, 129.

[7]Quoting either the Catechism or the Confession of Faith is, for all practical purposes, equal to quoting a text of Scripture in a "Confessional" Church. This is one of the major differences between a Baptist and a Presbyterian. A Baptist may set out his convictions in a confession of faith, but he will never treat his statements in the same way as a Presbyterian. Any individual Baptist church may write its own confession of faith, but not so a Presbyterian. This is what is meant by "Confessional Church." The Presbyterian Church (singular) is a "Confessional Church" where every individual local church is legally bound by every word in the *Westminster Confession of Faith*. Baptist churches (plural) are not a "Confessional Church" (denomination) in the above sense. A local Baptist church may question and reject certain things in a historic creed like the *Philadelphia Confession of Faith* and still be part of an Association of Baptist churches. Some present day Baptists seem to be forgetting this fact and are using historic Baptist Creeds to "prove" debatable points of doctrine. When a Baptist refuses to discuss a point of theology with the Bible and says, "The Creeds have spoken," he ceases to be a Baptist.

[8]R.L. Dabney, *Lectures in Systematic Theology*, Banner of Truth, p 354.

[9]It is essential that we do not confuse the "unity of the *Scriptures*" with what Covenant Theology calls the "unity of the *covenants*." We firmly believe in the unity of the Scriptures. However, we believe that unity is built around neither dispensations nor covenants. It is built around the promise and fulfillment of the Gospel in the person and work of our Lord Jesus Christ for His one elect people.

THREE

★ ★ ★

New Lawgiver or Master of Logic

"*Ye have heard that it was said by them of old time, Thou shalt not commit adultery: But I say unto you, That whosoever looketh on a women to lust after her hath already committed adultery in his heart.*"

Mt. 5:27 KJV

The actual words "Thou shalt not commit adultery" themselves are neither an addition to the Law of Moses nor a corruption of the teaching of Moses. Those are the exact words that God Himself wrote on the Tablets of Stone. Christ is using the exact words of the Seventh Commandment. How are we to understand this verse and the comparison that Christ makes between His teaching and the Seventh Commandment?

Commentators committed to Covenant Theology ignore the fact that the words Christ used are the very words written on the Tablets of Stone. Their whole position is built on treating these words as Rabbinical distortions of the commandment. This is not true for most other writers. William Hendriksen, himself an eminent Covenant Theologian, admits this fact in his comments on Mt. 5:21:

The formula, "You have heard that it was said" presents a difficulty, since the following phrase, considered by itself, can be translated either "*TO the men of long ago*"

(R.S.V.:" **TO** the men of old") or "***BY*** *the men of long ago.*" MANY translators and commentators prefer **TO**. **several others** favor **BY**. According to the first view Jesus meant that Moses in the law said something **TO** the fathers, and Jesus now "assumes a tone of superiority over the Mosaic **regulations** (A.T. Robertson, *Word Pictures*, Vol. 1, p 44). J. Jermias . . . expresses the same view in even stronger language when he states that "Jesus establishes a **new divine law** when he opposes his 'But I say unto you' to the Word of Scripture.[10]

Hendriksen then proceeds to show why he disagrees with the majority of commentators, including A.T. Robertson. It appears that Hendriksen's Covenant Theology is dictating what the text has to mean. He may be right and men like Robertson, one of the greatest Greek scholars in this century, may be wrong. It may be correct that all Christ is doing in the Sermon on the Mount is refuting the misunderstanding of the Pharisees. In such a case, the text would mean, "You have heard the distortions of the Seventh Commandment given by the Rabbinical fathers." However, such a view is arrived at only by *theological* implication and not by exegesis of the Biblical texts. It assumes that Christ is not actually quoting the Seventh Commandment even though He uses the exact words ("Thou shalt not commit adultery"), but rather that He is really referring to the Pharisee's faulty application of the commandment. This is an assumption not drawn from the text of Scripture. It literally puts words into the mouth of both Christ and the Pharisees that Scripture no where mentions. If Robertson is correct, and the text means that Moses spoke to the Israelites (or gave them the law), then Christ was indeed adding to the Law of Moses and raising it to a higher level. Covenant Theology must first assume that the only thing Christ is doing in the Sermon on the Mount is giving a true exposition of what Moses really meant and then say, "Christ may have used the identical words written on the Tablets of Stone but He was really quoting the Pharisees' bad interpretation of the Seventh Commandment." We repeat, that may be correct, but it cannot be proven from the text. It must be assumed purely on the basis presumed theology.

If Covenant Theology is correct, then Christ is not claiming any unique or personal authority in His own statement. He is claiming no more authority than Moses. Any philosopher could have refuted the Pharisees just as easily as Christ did. All Christ would be doing is appealing to logic as the foundation of His statement and accusing the Pharisees of ignorance for not applying correct reasoning to the stated truth in the commandment. Christ would be merely the latest and the greatest Rabbi giving the *true* interpretation of Moses. In no sense could He have been speaking with the authority of a new Lawgiver if this view is correct. Christ would be merely an *interpreter* of truth but in no sense a *giver of new truth*. He would be pointing us to Moses, and not to Himself, as our final authority. Christ would be merely rubber stamping Moses.

If the Covenant Theology view of law is correct, the question could not involve what the law actually *said*, since it did indeed say, "Thou shalt not commit adultery." The whole problem would merely revolve around what the Pharisees had supposedly added to the commandment. We repeat, if Christ is merely pointing out the Pharisees bad application of Moses, He would need no unique authority to say what He did if all that is involved is logic.

At this point it might be well to remind ourselves that the Word of God was not written just for Philosophers who know all of the rules of human logic. It was written for the common person, for housewives, truck drivers and others, so that they all might know how to live in real life situations. What the Bible actually says and what is "philosophically implied" may be two different things that only the philosophic elite seem to be capable of discerning. The Bible was written for understanding by both the educated and the uneducated.

Covenant Theologians use some fairly standard rules of logic for extracting additional truth out of specific commandments. We will quote from Thomas Watson as an example. In his book on the Ten Commandments, he gives eight rules to apply when studying a commandment. Here is a sample of Watson's rules:

> **RULE 2**. In the commandment . . . more is intended than is spoken.
>
> (1) Where any duty is commanded, the contrary sin is forbidden. When we are commanded to keep the Sabbath-day holy, we are forbidden to break the Sabbath. . . .

(2) Where any sin is forbidden, the contrary duty is commanded. When we are forbidden to take God's name in vain, the contrary duty, that we should reverence his name is enjoined. . . .

RULE 3. Where any sin is forbidden in the commandment, the occasion of it is also forbidden. Where murder is forbidden, envy and rash anger are forbidden, which may occasion it. . . .

RULE 5. Where greater sins are forbidden, lesser sins are also forbidden. Though no sin in its own nature is little, yet one may be comparatively less than the other. Where idolatry is forbidden, superstition is forbidden, or bringing innovation into God's worship, which he has not appointed.

RULE 7. God's law forbids not only the acting of sin in our own persons, but being accessory to, or having any hands in, the sins of others.
How and in what sense may we be said to partake of, and have a hand in the sins of others? . . .
We become accessory of the sins of others by not hindering them when it is in our power. *qui non prohibit cum potest, jubet* [The failure to prevent something, when it lies within your power, amounts to ordering it]. If a master of a family sees his servant break the Sabbath, or hears him swear, and does not use the **power** he has to   **suppress** him, he becomes **accessory** to his sin. . . . [11]

By applying rule 3 and rule 4, we can *logically* make the Seventh Commandment teach that it is a sin to lust in our heart. We agree that all of Watson's rules are logical and *philosophically* true. However, that is not the point at issue. Thomas Watson was not making "rules for the Church living in a pluralistic society," he was writing *laws* that would be used by both individuals and civil magistrates in a "Christian" nation. The laws governing the conscience were one and the same with the laws that were implemented with the power of the steel sword! Is it possible for a magistrate and a covenant of law to apply and punish the internal implications of an external commandment? Of course not. What is logically and philosophically true cannot always be turned into a law to be used in government. This was the heart of the issue between Roger Williams and John Cotton in the Massachusetts Bay Colony. It was the constant struggle whenever men tried to enforce the "first table of the Law" with the sword.

Only God Himself can judge the thoughts and intents of the heart. Imagine a judge putting a man in jail for day dreaming in his arm chair at home about either adultery or revenge on an enemy. The question is not philosophy and logic, but how the commandment was **applied** under the Law of Moses We may apply all of the logic to an external law that we choose to, but we cannot punish what is only *internally* implied in the commandment. Man can only measure and punish what can actually be observed.

Watson's rules may *all* be applicable for an individual seeking to understand how God looks at his heart and life. However, to use those rules to build a system of ethics with which to govern and punish men in society is disastrous. Rule 5 certainly applies to me as an individual in the sight of God. God can and does deal with me on the basis of what is in my heart. However, under a system of pure law, another human being can only deal with the overt acts simply because he cannot see my heart (Jer. 17:9). The Law of Moses could not deal with the heart or with motives simply because that is beyond the ability of a purely objective law.

We must not allow "logical deductions" of stated external laws to be turned into a system of governing and punishing people. Historically, this approach has often created great difficulty and brought reproach on the Church of Christ. This has come about when sincere men, like Thomas Watson, had the civil authority to make the "clear truth of God" (which they logically "deduced" as the "good and necessary consequence" of their Covenant Theology) into the law of the land. In reality, they were adding the commandments of men to the words of God by treating their logical deductions as texts of Scripture. "God spoke" the Puritan's *interpretation* of the Word of God just as clearly as He spoke the words recorded in Scripture.

Rule 7 is philosophically true. It is indeed our duty to do all in our power to keep other people from sinning and not be a "partaker of their wicked deeds." However, in order to apply this particular Rule in reference to the Sabbath (which Watson uses as an example) a master or magistrate must force everyone under his jurisdiction to attend worship services. For a master or magistrate to allow a person to sleep in on Sunday and not attend worship would clearly break Watson's rule and make the man in authority to be himself guilty of sinning in the sight of God for not using his "God given responsibility" to keep others from breaking God's clear commandment. "The Word of God clearly declares (according to my logical application) that it is our God ordained duty to *force* servants to go to church" was considered a "truth clearly revealed in the Word of God" according to Watson's rules of interpreting God's commandments.

It is easy to see why anyone using this method of interpretation can (most sincerely) literally "add the commandments of men to the Word of God" and then (again, most sincerely) commit nearly any form of persecution and tyranny and think that he is doing God a service as well as "helping his fellow man" because he sincerely "loves his soul?" The more sincere and devoted such a person is to that method of interpreting the Bible, the more dangerous and vicious he can be, and all in the name of "*honoring God's Holy Law*"? It would be literally impossible to avoid a system of legalistic despotism that would destroy Christian liberty and freedom of conscience. Under such a method of understanding and "sincerely" applying this kind of "Biblical truth," men could be, *and have been*, put to death in the cruelest manner, and those who killed them could sincerely believe that they did it out of love to God and His truth.

This is not caricature. All we have to do is read of the instances where the New England Puritans, and others, *did those very things.* If Watson is correct, then the Puritans were not only justified, they were actually duty bound by "God's Holy Law" to send the Sheriff around to get you out of bed and haul you off to the church service. God save us from men who use their version of "God's unchanging moral law" in this manner!

We simply must see that Law can only measure and punish outward acts of behavior. It cannot deal with the heart and inward motives. This is the heart of the issue that we are discussing in this book. This is always the real question when there is an honest discussion of "law and grace." The question is not whether a Christian is responsible to obey "objective laws" or simply follow an emotion called "love." The question concerns whether the Law of Moses, *even correctly understood*, can deal with the heart and motives, or whether this can only be accomplished by the indwelling Holy Spirit given at Pentecost.

The Tablets of Stone cannot be the foundation of the Christian's rule of life. However, this is *not* because the Tablets contain "laws" and the Christian is somehow against laws just because he is "not under law but under grace." That is nonsense. Nor is the problem that the Law of Moses is too high a standard for a Christian today. The heart of the difficulty is that the laws on the Tablets of Stone are *not high and spiritual enough* for a full fledged son of God living under the New Covenant. The Tablets of Stone are great for the purpose for which God designed and gave them. However, conviction of sin that leads to justification by faith is not the goal of the laws of Christ given to people who are *already justified.*[12]

Once we settle how and why the commandments were applied under the law covenant, then the next obvious question concerns whether Christ, in the Sermon on the Mount, is making new and higher demands based entirely on grace or merely giving a lesson in logic by exposing the Pharisees' misunderstanding of the Law of Moses. It seems clear that the texts are showing that Christ was giving new and higher truth. In essence Christ was saying:

> "Moses was quite correct under a covenant of law. However, my Ekklesia is not going to be 'under the law but under grace.' In the kingdom of Grace, the law will be written on the heart. The Holy Spirit will indwell every believer as the new and personal *Pedagogue* sent to take My place. He will point every believer to the Cross and not to a sword, and this will move their hearts to love and obey *My new (objective) laws!"*

This is the heart of the issue. This is the difference between the Old Covenant of law that governed the nation of Israel and the New Covenant of grace under which the Church lives. Both covenants have objective laws or commandments, but the laws of the New Covenant make higher demands because they appeal to the cross. "Thou shalt not commit adultery" has a higher and deeper meaning when applied by Christ under the New Covenant than it could have ever had when merely written on stone. The appeal to the cross is a higher motive, and the ground of both the motive and the duties enjoined are embodied in the truth and power of grace that comes to us through the New Covenant established by the redemptive work of Christ.

The correct way to approach Mt. 5:27 is *just let it mean exactly what it says.* Let it really contrast the difference between rule under covenant law and rule under grace without in any way suggesting that Moses and the law were "wrong." Let Christ be truly greater than Moses without demeaning or depreciating either Moses or his law. Allow Christ to make laws that are morally higher and more spiritual than the Law of Moses. Don't push the Sermon on the Mount forward into the "kingdom age" under the pretense that it "opposes grace." And likewise, don't try to push Christ's new law back into the Old Testament by using the logical deductions of a theological system that in practice takes priority over the contextual meaning of Bible texts. Let the Lord Jesus Christ have the right and ability to give His New Covenant people new and higher truth than Moses ever gave to Israel!

Regardless of what view we take, we must admit to certain facts. If Christ is only showing the true intention of the Law of Moses in Mt. 5:27 as it concerns adultery, then He is claiming neither Scriptural authority nor any unique personal authority for His statement. He is merely showing the Pharisees their mistake in logic. Christ does not quote the Old Testament Scriptures in His contrast nor does He state that He is refuting a "wrong interpretation" of Moses. If Christ is only refuting a distortion of Moses by showing what Moses actually taught, then why does He not quote from another part of the law and prove what Moses really did mean? This is what Christ did in Matthew four with the Devil. When the Devil misapplied an Old Testament Scripture, our Lord responded by quoting an Old Testament text that clarified what God really meant. Would He not have done the same thing here if the Law of Moses taught the same thing that He was teaching? This would be doubly appropriate if Christ's primary purpose in the Sermon on the Mount was only to correctly interpret Moses.

We must see and accept the truth that Christ is actually contrasting the difference between a legal rule and a gracious rule (And *both kinds of rule* were ordained by God in their own time). This passage (Mt. 5:32,32) means that Christ is not only appealing directly to His own authority as the Son of God to interpret and apply Old Testament Scripture in a new and higher manner, He is also giving *new Scriptures* that contain *new truth*. Christ is declaring His own authority as the new Lawgiver. He is neither appealing to the Old Testament Scriptures for either His authority or for His message nor is He merely using good logic to prove His point. Christ is literally giving us new and additional Scriptures that reveal new and higher truth not found anywhere in Moses! This is a key point in this whole discussion and the bottom line is nothing less than the full and final authority of Christ as the new and final Lawgiver.

One of the weaknesses of Covenant Theology is treating the New Testament Scriptures as if they were nothing more than the correct interpretation and application of the Old Testament Scriptures. Even Christ Himself cannot give any real *new moral laws* under that system of theology. However, the New Testament Scriptures clearly show that Christ is more than just an interpreter and applier of Old Testament law. He is the Giver of *new law*. He is the new Moses as well as the second Adam.

We simply must see Christ as "That *Prophet*" that was to replace Moses as God's Lawgiver. To view Christ as merely the "true interpreter of Moses" is to destroy Christ's unique authority and reduce Him to being only equal to Moses or else the greatest student and interpreter that Moses ever had. The New Testament Scriptures will not allow us to exalt Moses and minimize the authority of our Lord Jesus Christ in such a manner? Moses dare not be the ultimate and final authority over either Christ or His disciples.

The essence of Christ's claim in the Sermon on the Mount, as well as Paul's clear declaration in his epistles, is that Moses has been done away and replaced by the new and final Lawgiver. We repeat, in no sense does this mean that Christ is contradicting Moses. Christ is not destroying Moses, but He is most certainly replacing Moses in the same sense that He replaced Aaron. We do not demean Moses anymore than we demean Aaron when we emphasize that both of their ministries are done away because they are fulfilled in Christ. We do not minimize or cast off a moral law by allowing Christ to raise that law to a higher level.

[10]*Gospel of Matthew*—NT *Commentary*, by William Hendriksen, Baker Book House, p 295.

[11]Thomas Watson, *The Ten Commandments*, Banner of Truth, p 44-48.

[12]We have developed this truth in The Tablets of Stone. This book is available from Crowne Publications, Inc.

★ ★ ★

FOUR

Justice and Punishment Versus Pity and Mercy

*Y*ou have heard that it was said, 'Eye for eye, and *tooth for tooth.' **But I tell you**, Do not resist an evil person. If someone strikes you on the right cheek, turn to him the other also. And if someone wants to sue you and take your tunic, let him have your cloak as well. If someone forces you to go one mile, go with him two miles. Give to the one who asks you, and do not turn away from the one who wants to borrow from you.*

Matthew 5:38-42

Suppose we grant that Christ was only "giving the true intention of Moses" in Mt. 5:27 (and we grant that was one thing He was doing), that approach will not explain the verses just quoted. In Mt. 5:38-42 Christ has to be contrasting Himself and His teaching with Moses and the Law. However, it is a *contrast* that is not a *contradiction*. In this passage, Christ is neither correcting a faulty interpretation of Moses nor is He pointing out an additional text in the Old Testament Scriptures. In Mt. 5:38-42, Christ is clearly contrasting Himself with Moses! This is the new Lawgiver laying down rules for people living "under grace" that were not only impossible to be given to those "under the Law," but in some cases, as we shall see in a moment, would have been *unlawful* under the Law!

25

Look carefully at the texts quoted above. If we accept these words in their normal meaning, and apply the same kind of reasoning that we use when we interpret the rest of Scripture, then we are forced to admit the following facts:

First, nowhere in the Old Covenant legislation can anything be found that is similar to Christ's clear statements. If all Christ is doing is showing what Moses really taught, and if Moses did indeed teach the same thing that Christ said in His contrast, then why did not Christ simply quote the Old Testament texts that proved His point. As we mentioned earlier, why did He not do with the Pharisees as He did with Satan in Matthew four? When Satan misapplied an Old Testament text, Christ quoted another Old Testament text that proved Satan was wrong.

We can no more read the words of Mt. 5:39-42 back into the Law of Moses than the Pharisee could make the Old Covenant law teach "hate your enemies." We can find in the Old Testament Scriptures examples of men's actions proving that the principle of grace was operating in their hearts, but those actions were not, and could not, have been *demanded* under a covenant of law[13]. We can find many proverbs and moral laws in the Old Testament Scriptures that gave clear objective rules of conduct to an Israelite. However, we cannot find Christ's new commandments that are based on pure grace anywhere in the Law of Moses.

Second, the "greater includes the lesser" principle cannot apply here. The law of Christ that says "turn the other cheek" cannot be either a "greater" or "lesser" application of the "eye for eye" principle of justice. Likewise, not "resisting evil" cannot possibly be logically deduced from the "eye for eye and tooth for tooth" justice of Moses. The one is the true application of Biblical justice and the other is the true application of Biblical grace. Neither the twisted logic of the Pharisees, nor Watson's rules of interpreting commandments, can make this passage be anything other than a clear contrast between the severe but just Law of Moses and the gracious (and also "just" because of Calvary) law of Christ.

We may be a bit reluctant to admit it, but if anyone other than Christ Himself would have made these statements, we would automatically accuse them of "adding to" the Word of God. In reality, that is exactly what Christ is doing, *and He has every right to do so!* Let me once again add quickly that Christ is not saying

that Moses was wrong and needed to be corrected. Christ is saying, "Moses was perfectly correct in stating and applying the principle of 'eye for eye and tooth for tooth' justice under a system
of *covenant law*, but I am stating and *demanding* that My disciples apply much *higher laws* under a system of *grace*."

Must we make the Law of Moses to be equal in all of its parts
to the teaching of our Lord Jesus Christ in order to protect our
particular view of the "moral law" of God?[14] Why do men insist
that Christ's law must be on a one and one equal par with the
Law of Moses? Why is our insistence that the laws that Christ gave
are higher and greater than the Law of Moses pictured by some
men as a "denial of the holy law of God?" What is wrong with
making Christ to be a new and greater Lawgiver as long as we
give Moses the same place and respect that the Scriptures give
him? Are we so married to Moses that we must insist on making
him equal to Christ? Or even worse, must we, like Dabney, exalt
Moses even *above* Christ? God forbid!

The answer to all of these "why" questions is really quite
simple. Some men realize that *the basic pre-supposition of their
theology is contradicted by what is being said*. If Christ gives
any law that is different in any real sense from the Law of Moses,
then we have *two different canons of conduct for Israel and the
Church*, and that is not possible in Covenant Theology. If Christ
really established a New Covenant with some new laws, and that
New Covenant replaced the Old Covenant (Tables of Stone) given
at Sinai (Ex. 34:1,27,28; Dt. 4:13-18), then the foundation of
Covenant Theology's "one covenant with two administrations"
is destroyed. When the very foundations of our system of theology is challenged, it is easier to hurl labels like "antinomian" or
build straw men than it is to calmly discuss the actual words of
Scripture. This book is concerned with Scripture alone and not
"theological *deductions*." We are exegeting Bible verses and not
logically "deducing" things out of theological statements.

Moses and Christ simply must teach the same laws in order
for Covenant Theology to be true. In the eyes of a Covenant
Theologian, Contrasting "the laws of Christ" to the "Law of
Moses" is nothing less than a heresy that attacks both the "unity
of the covenants" and "the perpetuity of the moral law of God."
For anyone to teach that Christ has established a new and different covenant that literally replaces the Old Covenant is to

destroy the basic foundation upon which Covenant Theology's "one covenant/two administrations" rests.

Anyone that holds to Covenant Theology is frightened to death of making any kind of contrast between "law" and "grace" only because such a contrast undermines his basic presupposition. The Apostle Paul will boldly contrast *"law and grace"* (Rom. 6:14), and Jesus will do the same (John 1:17). However, a consistent Covenant Theologian will always contrast "law and *gospel"* instead of "law and *grace"* in spite of the fact that the Word of God often contrasts law with "grace" and never contrasts law with "gospel."

We simply dare not treat the words used by the Holy Spirit in Scripture the way some writers and preachers do when those words obviously will not fit into our particular theological mold. When the writer of Hebrews emphatically states that a New Covenant has replaced an *Old* Covenant, we are denying every rule of true exegesis by saying, "but the writer does not really mean there are two *different* covenants. He really means there is a new *administration* of the *one and same covenant of grace that Moses was under."* If this is true, then the Holy Spirit can be charged with the following: (1) He said what He actually did not mean; and (2) He did not say what He actually did mean.

It is absolutely impossible to hold such a view and let either the words of Christ in the Sermon on the Mount or Paul's emphatic statements concerning law and grace mean anything close to what they actually say. When both Christ and Paul contrast "law" and "grace" in a purely covenantal sense, how dare we say, "They really don't mean what they actually say." When Jesus clearly contrasts His teaching with that of Moses, we dare not attempt to make them both say the thing.

It is obvious that personal theology affects the way a writer or a preacher will approach a particular passage of Scripture. This is especially true in a passage such as Mt. 5:38-42. The following quotation by Greg Bahnsen is the consistent Covenant Theology view of the "true" purpose of the Sermon on the Mount:

> Christ's **primary** concern at this point [Mt. 5:17-48] was the validity and meaning of the **older** Testamental law. From the antitheses listed in verse 21-48 we see that Christ was concerned to show how the **meaning of the Law was being distorted** (and thus its fine points overlooked).

> These radical commands (Mt. 5:21-48) **do NOT** supersede the **older** Testamental law; they **illustrate and explain it. . . . In six antitheses between His teaching and the scribal interpretations Christ demonstrates His confirmation** of the **Older** Testamental law. . . .
>
> So we see in Matthew 5:21-48 examples of how Christ **confirms** the **Older** Testamental law and reproves the **Pharisaical use of it;** the antitheses are case law application of the principle enunciated in Matthew 5:17-20. Christ did not come to abrogate the law; far from it! He confirmed it in **full measure**, thereby condemning scribal legalism and showing us the pattern of our **Christian sanctification.**[15]

Bahnsen's book contains 619 pages and *not one time* in the whole book does he say "Old Testament." He always, as in the above quotation, says "Older Testamental law." Bahnsen does this deliberately to demonstrate as forcefully as possible that there is no such thing as a *new* and an *Old* Covenant. There is only an *older* and a *newer version* of the *one and same* covenant of grace. We wonder why the writers of both the Old Testament Scriptures and New Testament Scriptures never once use either the word "Older" or the phrase "Older Testamental law" when they talk about the Old Covenant?

Why will Bahnsen (1) refuse to use the very words that the Holy Spirit used, and (2) constantly use words that the Holy Spirit never used even once? Does, or does not, the Word of God clearly state in plain words that there is indeed both a New and an Old Covenant, and further, that the New Covenant has replaced and done away with the Old Covenant (Heb. 8:6-13)? And where does the Word of God even *one time* talk about "two (an "older" and a "newer") *administrations*" of one and the same "*Testamental law*?

Bahnsen assumes that Christ's "primary purpose" in the Sermon on the Mount is to give the *true* understanding of the Mosaic law and refute the Pharisee's distortions of that law. Christ is not asserting Himself as a *new Lawgiver* but only enforcing the law as already given by Moses. The primary purpose of Christ is to firmly establish the permanent "validity and [true] meaning" of the "Older Testamental law" in the conscience of the Christian.

Christ can never give new or higher laws.

Covenant Theology must insist that Christ, in the Sermon on the Mount, is sending the New Covenant believer back to Moses for *both the foundation and the content* of all of his moral instructions. In reality, Christ is merely rubber stamping the Old Covenant and its laws, and then firmly planting Moses in the Christian's conscience as the God-ordained supervisor of our sanctification. In Bahnsen's words, Christ is sending the New Covenant believer back to Moses as the *permanent* God-ordained "pattern of our Christian sanctification."

In other words, good logic applied to Moses can give us all of the moral teaching and spiritual application that we need in our sanctification. The New Testament Scriptures and the advent of the Holy Spirit to indwell believers merely help to explain and confirm what Moses really meant. Covenant Theology is telling us that there is *nothing* that we need to know in order to be truly holy that is not found in a *correct understanding of Moses.* Every moral duty of a Christian must be a direct outgrowth and application of one of the Ten Commandments.

The texts in the Sermon on the Mount are saying something entirely different. Our Lord is doing more than just rubber stamping Moses and planting Moses' authority in the Christian's conscience as a *Pedagogue.* Such an interpretation is arrived at only by applying logic to a theological system of which you already convinced. A previously held system of theology dictated this approach and not an exegesis of the texts of Scripture.

Mt. 5:38-42 teaches that Christ is deliberately contrasting a legal rule by pure law (which is right and good under a covenant of law) and a gracious rule (which is higher and better but only possible under a covenant of grace). We do not believe that Pink, Bahnsen, or any writer that follows their approach, can do justice to the actual words of Christ in the Sermon on the Mount. They cannot do so and be consistent with the "one covenant and two administrations" view.

In Mt. 5:38-42, Christ is asserting His authority as the New Lawgiver to lay down the rules for the kingdom of grace under which His disciples were to live. He was actually *adding* to the rules and the revelation that God gave to His Old Covenant people but in no sense was He *contradicting* that revelation as if it were *wrong.* Christ was saying some things that were literally impossible for Moses to say or apply as long as the law covenant stood in force. Grace can and does demand of believers living under grace things that would have been, in some cases, contrary to the Law of Moses. If Moses would have demanded what Christ is demanding of His disciples in Mt. 5:39-42, then Moses would have contradicted Moses. Likewise, there are some things that must be maintained under a system of pure law governing *unbelievers* that cannot be demanded under a system of grace that governs *believers*.

Before we get bogged down in side tracks, let us make sure we know exactly what Moses meant in the law when he said "eye for eye and tooth for tooth." The failure to understand what Moses actually said is the primary cause of getting mixed up. Once we see why this principle was given in the Law of Moses to govern a physical nation of sinners, it is easy to see why it cannot be applied under grace in governing a *spiritual* nation of *saints*. We will see that a Christian is commanded in the Sermon on the Mount to do things that an Israelite could never have been commanded to do under the Law of Moses.

Many writers make unwarranted assumptions at this point about what the Old Testament Scriptures meant without actually exegeting the texts. They invariably assume that the primary purpose of the "eye for eye" law was to check the tendency for revenge. The following quotation by Martyn Lloyd-Jones is a typical comment on Mt. 5:38-42:

> The **main intent** of the Mosaic legislation was to **control excesses**. In this case in particular, it was to **control anger** and violence and the **desire for revenge**. . . . Now this tendency was manifesting itself amongst the children of Israel and there are examples of it given in the Old Testament literature. The object, therefore, of this Mosaic legislation was to control and reduce this utterly **chaotic** condition **to a certain amount of order**.[16]

With all due respect to one of the greatest men of God in this generation, such a statement simply is not being fair with the actual data in the Old Testament Scriptures. It seems impossible that anyone can carefully study the Old Testament passages dealing with "eye for eye and tooth for tooth" and then claim that "the *main* intent" of those laws was "to control anger and violence and the desire for revenge."[17]

We are not suggesting that the above quote is saying something that is totally false. *One* of the purposes of the "eye for eye" law may have been to restrain the urge for revenge on the part of an offended individual even though such an idea is not stated in any of the texts in the Old Testament Scriptures. However, when that is made the only reason, or even the *primary* reason, then we are reading our theology into the Scriptures and ignoring what the Biblical texts themselves actually say.

Let us examine the three Old Testament texts that speak of the "eye for eye" law and see if Lloyd-Jones is correct concerning the "main" purpose of this legislation. We will begin with the first instance when this particular law was actually given:

> *If men who are fighting hit a pregnant woman and she gives birth prematurely but there is no serious injury, the offender must be fined whatever the woman's husband demands and the court allows. **But if there is serious injury**, you are to take life for life, eye for eye, tooth for tooth, hand for hand, burn for burn, wound for wound, bruise for bruise.*
>
> Ex. 21:22-25

This passage shows that the "eye for eye" law was given at the same time the Ten Commandments were given. It was part of the "Book of the Covenant" that included the Decalogue. The Ten Commandments, or the actual covenant itself (Ex. 34:1,27,28), was given in Ex. 20. Ex. 21-23 applied the covenant to some real life situations. All of Ex. 20 through Ex. 23, including the Ten Commandments, were written down and called "The Book of The Covenant" (Ex. 24:7,8). The Book of the Covenant was read aloud to all of the people and they verbally responded and entered into covenant with God. Moses then sprinkled them with blood.

> *Then he [Moses] took the Book of the Covenant [which contained Ex. 20-23] and read it in the hearing of the people. And they said, "All that the Lord has said we will do, and be obedient." And Moses took the blood, sprinkled it on the people, and said, "Behold, the blood of the covenant which the Lord has made with you according*

to all these words.

Ex. 24:7,8

It is misleading to say that the "object of this legislation (Ex. 21:22-25) was to control and reduce this utterly chaotic condition to a certain amount of order." The text itself does not say or suggest this. In actual fact, the nation had just, at that very moment, come into existence as a nation or "body politic." At that point in time there were no "chaotic conditions" that needed to be brought under control. God was laying down a system of justice and putting it into the "constitution" of the nation that was just being established. The "Book of the Covenant" was to be the basis of how that society was going to be governed. The "eye for eye" law is just as much the "moral law of God" for Israel's rule of life as the Ten Commandments.[18]

The purpose of the "eye for eye" law was basically the same as the laws of our land today. As we shall see in a later reference to the "eye for eye" law, the primary intent was not, as Lloyd-Jones stated, to be sure that sin was not punished too much, but rather *to be certain that sin was actually punished.* The second stated purpose of this law was to set an example that would act as a deterrent to others. The mandatory carrying out of this law was to be an example to others as a means of keeping them from committing the same sins. We deliberately used the word "sin" instead of "crime" in this paragraph because these acts were being dealt with as violations of God's covenant (sins) and not just as crimes against society. We are talking about a physical theocracy that was governed directly by the Law of God. There is no such nation today nor do the New Testament Scriptures encourage us to set one up.

A careful study of Ex. 21:22-25 will clearly demonstrate that it is misleading to stress that the "eye for eye and tooth for tooth" law was given primarily to curb revenge. That may or may not have been one facet of the law. The primary purpose was to establish a just basis and method for making sure that sin was actually punished. The primary point of the "eye for eye" law was not first aimed at protecting the offending party from the anger and revenge of a fellow man. The "eye for eye" law was given to make sure that the offending party was *justly punished for his sin against God and His law.* This law was more than "social justice." It was part of the legal covenant that established the special relationship of the nation of Israel with God. The "eye for eye" law dealt with *sin against God* not just crime against a neighbor. This is why mercy was not even allowed, let alone commanded, in this legislation.

In their zeal to protect Moses from charges of cruel and inhumane legislation, we fear some good men have not allowed the Old Testament Scriptures to mean what they actually say. They do to God's laws in the Old Testament Scriptures exactly what many modern liberals do to our penal system when they try to make the *primary* purpose of prison to be rehabilitation. Most people are eager to see everything possible being done to teach and train people in prison so that they are enabled to be kept from returning to prison once they are released. We agree that such a policy is to the ultimate benefit of both society and the criminal. All of us should encourage and support every such effort. However, we must not lose sight of the fact that the *primary* reason for the prison's existence is the punishment of crime and the protection of society and not the rights or rehabilitation of the criminal. The same was even more true in Israel under the Law of Moses. The primary purpose of the "eye to eye" law was to punish sin against God and not just to be sure that punishment was not extreme. The justice and honor of God was the goal and not the right or protection of the criminal.

Ex. 21:22-25 shows a clear distinction between the method of punishment when the injury *was not serious* as compared to when it *was serious.* In the first instance the offended party set the fine and got whatever the court allowed. Not only was vengeance curbed, but presumably the offended party could have dismissed the whole thing and "forgiven" the offender. The "eye for eye" part did not come into play until the injury was serious, and then the commandment was "you are to take life for life, eye for eye, etc . . . " (vs 23). Neither the offended individual nor the judges any longer had any control over the terms of the punishment when the injury was serious. God Himself set the exact terms of the punishment in such cases. It was then a duty of the court and justice to enforce God's law of "eye for eye and tooth for tooth" without pity.

At this point, the purpose was not at all concerned with curbing anger but with vindicating God's law. Actually, the "eye for eye" part of the law did not in any way apply to curbing revenge in this text. Both Lloyd-Jones and Pink miss the whole point of this Old Testament Scripture. The importance of this will be developed in a moment.

Let us look at the second instance of the "eye for eye and tooth for tooth" law. The emphasis is mine:

> *If anyone takes the life of a human being, he must be put to death. Anyone who takes the life of someone's animal* **must make restitution**—*life for life. If anyone injures his neighbor, whatever he has done* **must be done** *to him: fracture for fracture, eye for eye, tooth for tooth. As he has injured the other, so he* **is to be injured.**
>
> Lev. 24:17-20

Again the context shows that this is an application of the covenant law of God and not just "social justice." In this text forgiveness and dismissal of the punishment was not possible. Regardless of how deep a man's repentance may have been, there was no provision for mercy or forgiveness in this particular law. This was "covenant breaking" and *punishment was mandatory*, and the *exact amount* of punishment was clearly prescribed by God. We should thank God that we do not live under such a system. We should also oppose every attempt by sincere but misguided people who may attempt to set up such a system.

In the verses immediately preceding this commandment (Lev. 24:10-16), Moses is directed to stone a man to death who had blasphemed God. The justification for such punishment is stated in verses 17-20 which we just quoted. In verse 23, there is a return to the blasphemer and the text says, "*Then Moses spoke to the Israelites,* and they took the blasphemer outside the camp and stoned him. . . ."

At least three things are clear in this passage:

One: The stated purpose of the legislation was positive and not negative. Enforcing of the "eye for eye" law was not "to keep someone's anger under control and limit punishment," but rather to assure that deserved punishment was actually exercised. It is impossible to read "the MAIN intent of this law was to restrain anger and revenge" into Lev. 24:17-20. Such an interpretation destroys the true meaning of the text.

Two: We cannot divide up the various crimes mentioned in this text and say or imply that punishment was mandatory in some cases but not mandatory in others. The principle of "eye for eye and tooth for tooth" is applied across the board. Capital punishment was mandatory for murder and injuries done to the neighbor had to be punished in like degree. Likewise, there is nothing in the text to indicate the possibility of a "negotiated settlement" where the charge could be dropped or the specific punishment be determined by either the offended party or the judges. Everything was clearly specified by God's law. It was "eye for eye" across the board to insure that just punishment for every violation was actually carried out and had nothing to do with "curbing anger and the desire for revenge." We must accept what the text actually says.

Three: There is nothing either cruel or inhumane in such a system of justice if it is carried out consistently. Its end is the glory of God and the good of society. It will help restrain anger *before the first eye* is put out!

There is nothing at all in this whole chapter, especially the verses just quoted, that would indicate the primary purpose of the "eye for eye" legislation was to "curb revenge." We must not allow either our theological system or the taunts of the liberals to force us into misrepresenting what God's Word clearly says. This text shows that if you curse God then "eye for eye" justice assures that you will be cursed by God—and verse 19 clearly shows that the same "eye for eye" punishment was just as mandatory in all of the cases being discussed simply because they were all *sins against God's covenant law*. There is nothing in the text about "*you may*, if you choose," but it does clearly say, "*you shall*" because of justice. The magistrate was an executor of God's justice and not a referee controlling men's anger.

It would be no more legalistic to carry out the punishments in the latter part of verse 19 than it was when capitol punishment was exacted for blasphemy in verse 23; the reason being that God's covenant law was being considered and not just another human being. If it were only the latter, then vengeance may be involved and need to be controlled, but if we think in terms of sin against the law of God that is a different story. We are not talking about a "social contract" when we discuss Lev. 24:17-25; we are talking about the covenant law of God that established and governed a theocratic nation. It is not "accidental" that three instances in the Old Testament Scriptures of stoning to death involved "merely" picking up sticks on the Sabbath, blasphemy, and taking a few garments and gold as spoils of war. Were those things "small crimes" against society or "wicked sins" against God?

By the way, which is the most cruel and which is the most humane in the following situations: allowing teenagers month after month to terrorize and rob elderly widows of their food stamps and welfare checks and thus deprive them of food and heat, or cutting off the hands of a few of the repeat offenders who are doing the robbing? We seem to be able to watch innocent victims go through continual inhumane treatment at the hands of criminals (Is going hungry and possibly dying of malnutrition "inhumane"?) while refusing to in any way exercise the kind of punishment that might stop those consistently responsible for such crimes under the pretense that such punishment is "cruel and inhumane." What do we call the treatment that criminals give to their helpless victims—merely "unfortunate"? Did you ever wonder how long it was before anyone blasphemed God after the fellow was stoned to death in Lev. 24?

The final use of the "eye for eye" justice in the Old Testament Scriptures makes this last point even more clear:

> *If a malicious witness takes the stand to accuse a man of a crime, the two men involved in the dispute must stand in the presence of the Lord before the priest and the judges who are in office at the time. The judges must make a thorough investigation, and if the witness proves to be a liar, giving false testimony against his brother, then* **do to him** *as he intended to do to his brother. You* **must purge evil from among you.** *The rest of the people will hear of this and be afraid, and never again will such an evil thing be done among you.* **Show no pity:** *life for life, eye for eye, tooth for tooth, hand for hand, foot for foot.*

> Dt. 19:16-21

Notice carefully the following things in this passage:

One: There could be no *pity*, justice had to prevail. The specified punishment of "eye for eye and tooth for tooth" was mandatory if the crime was proven. It is impossible to make this

passage teach or imply that the *main purpose* (or even a secondary purpose) of the "eye for eye" law was to curb anger and
revenge and protect the offending party from too much punishment. If the liar's accusation would have resulted in the accused
party being put to death, then the magistrate *had no choice* but
to punish the liar with death.

Two: The *amount* of punishment in this situation was not
in the hands of either the individual offended or the court.
Carrying out the prescribed punishment was the only thing that
was in the hands of the court and justice, and it was the judges'
duty to "purge the evil" out of society. The glory of God, the
integrity of His law, and the spiritual good of God's nation was
the whole object of this legislation.

Three: The text, vs 19-21, shows that this particular instance
was dealing with a false witness (again, one of the Ten Words),
and the false witness was to be given the *exact penalty* that the
other man would have gotten if the lies had not been exposed.
It was literally a mandatory "eye for eye."

Four: The sole purpose of the "eye for eye and tooth for
tooth" law was the punishment of sin to demonstrate the justice
of God and the need for holiness. The sure and just punishment
of breaking God's law would act as a deterrent to other would-
be blasphemers and false witnesses. Neither the "rights" of the
false witness nor the "pity" of the man lied about were factors
in what had to be done. It was the law of God that had been dis-
obeyed, and it was the law of God that was now in charge of
the situation, and the specified punishment had to be honored
in judgement.

In all honesty, can we believe that either Lloyd-Jones or Pink
gives a true picture of what the Old Testament Scriptures are saying in the "eye for eye" legislation? Can we make any of those
passages teach that "the *main* intention" of the "eye for eye and
tooth for tooth" law was to restrain "the urge for revenge?" We
think not.

We mentioned earlier that we would return to the fact that
the "eye for eye and tooth for tooth" punishment was not in the
hands of the individual but the court. Every writer that takes the
view expressed by Lloyd-Jones and Pink will make much of this
fact. It is the method used to try to prove that Christ is not making a contrast between either Moses and Himself or law and grace.

These writers teach that Christ was accusing the Pharisees of twisting the Law of Moses by urging individuals to take this law into their own hands and personally exact justice rather than allow the court and judges to handle the situation. This of course fits well with the idea that the *main purpose* of the "eye for eye" law was only to curb anger and revenge. However, it does not fit into the texts of Scripture. The following quotation from Lloyd-Jones typifies this view:

> But perhaps the most important thing is that this enactment was **not given to the individual,** but rather to the judges who were responsible for law and order amongst the individuals. . . . It was the judges who were to see to it that it was eye for eye and a tooth for tooth and **no more.** The legislation was for them, **not for private individuals**. . . . As far as the teaching of the Pharisees and scribes is concerned, their main trouble was that they tended to ignore entirely the fact that this teaching was for the **judges only.** They made it a matter of **personal application.**[19]

Again, we do not question that what has just been quoted may contain an element of truth. However, to make this stand for either the whole truth or even the primary application of Christ's teaching in this passage is to miss the real truth that Christ is declaring. By demanding that His disciples as *individuals* should respond to injustice in a gracious way, Christ is actually doing the very thing that Lloyd-Jones says was the *main problem* of the Pharisees. Christ is NOT applying *His* teaching to the *magistrates* and telling them how they are to apply Moses. But He is telling *individual Christians* how they, as individuals, are to act under His new gracious law.

Christ, in this passage, is:

(1.) telling the individual Christian not to live according to the Old Covenant "eye for eye" law of retaliation;

(2.) taking the responsibility for these actions totally out of the hands of the court and the judges;

(3.) placing the responsibility for the correct response entirely on the *conscience of the individual Christian;*

(4.) forcing the Christian *as an individual* to think and to respond in terms of pure grace instead of law.

Christ is **not** teaching that a Christian should "follow the Law of Moses" and act in justice but not punish *too much*. He is teaching that a Christian must be gracious towards a brother and not *punish at all*. The magistrate has no function in the situation that Christ is describing. In no sense are we saying, "Away with the magistrate." We are merely saying that Christ, in this passage, is giving instructions to the Church and not to society. The Sermon on the Mount does not replace the Law of Moses as the new rules for society. He is telling individual Christians that they should no longer determine their attitudes and actions by law and justice but by grace and love.

Christ is saying things in these verses that the Law of Moses could never have said. He is: (1.) putting our duty and behavior as New Covenant believers into the context of pure grace instead of law and justice; (2.) He is making our response to certain types of injustice to be a matter of our individual conscience; (3.) Christ is demanding that we live under the new laws that He is giving; (4.) He is holding us accountable as individuals to personally take *His new laws into our own hands!* Christ, is commanding us to respond in pure grace and pity in the same situation that, under the law, *had to be dealt* with *without pity* by an "eye for eye" justice.

Under "law", individual conscience cannot rule nor can love ever supersede law. This is true of the actions of both the offended party and the judge. The only question is, "What does the law say and require?" Under the Law of Moses the only answer was "an eye for eye." Under grace the exact opposite is true. The individual's conscience is bound to Christ by love, and pure justice may not supersede the love of Christ. Love will never contradict law, but, unlike the mandatory nature of law, under grace there is an option to act in love and pity instead of pure justice. In no sense is this vilifying law, it is merely showing the great superiority of grace.

We repeat, in the Sermon on the Mount, Christ is demanding (making it a law) that the individual disciple in His kingdom of grace do the very thing which Lloyd-Jones accused the Pharisees of urging their disciples to do.

The demand that Christ is here making on a child of His kingdom is simply not possible for any magistrate or court (including Moses and all of his laws) to make on one of their subjects. Christ is once more showing us the vital difference between legal rules under a covenant of law and gracious rules under a covenant of grace. Both methods of rule are "holy, just and good." But the one is superior and better than the other because it is rooted in the New Covenant and energized by the indwelling Holy Spirit. Both methods of rule have clear objective standards and in many instances the moral content of the rules may be the same. However, the Law of Moses can neither demand nor produce the kind of behavior that Christ is demanding in the Sermon on the Mount. The Holy Spirit can, and does, produce that kind of behavior in the life of New Covenant believers.

This whole thing is so simple once we understand that there has been a change of covenants. We are not in any way demeaning Moses and God's Holy Law given through him when we exalt Christ and His new laws. The whole New Testament demonstrates the weakness and inability of the Law of Moses as a covenant when compared with the New Covenant in the blood of Christ. Is the writer of Hebrews (Heb. 8:6-13), or Paul (II Cor. 3:6-11), demeaning the Old Covenant or Moses when they show why both Moses and his law covenant had to be replaced with a new and "better" covenant?

The real problem with the Old Covenant (Tablets of Stone) could not be solved by merely giving an interpretation of its "true spiritual meaning." The whole covenant itself had to be replaced by a new and better covenant that would make certain that God's true goal would be reached (Heb. 8:6-13; 10:1-18). The New Testament Scriptures declare with great joy (John 1:17; Heb. 10:16-18; I Cor. 11:23-26) that both the goal of God and the expectations and hopes of the true believer living under the Old Covenant (Jer. 31:33,34; I Pet. 1:10-12) have finally been realized. In the establishment of the New Covenant through the finished work of Christ, the fulfillment of the promises have finally been realized (Heb. 11:13,39).

Again, we are not saying that there was no gracious behavior exhibited in the Old Testament Scriptures. The incident mentioned earlier concerning Abraham and Lot was surely "turning the other cheek" in a very real sense. Joseph's treatment of his brothers is equal to anything in the New Testament Scriptures except the behavior of our Lord Himself. We are saying that a covenant of law would be contradicting itself if it *demanded* (legislated as law) such behavior. Law cannot legislate "eye for eye" and also demand that you "turn the other cheek" in the same legal code without having a self-contradiction. Joseph would not have been allowed, let alone commanded, to forgive his brothers and spare them from death if the Mosaic law of "eye for eye" had been in force at that time. They would have been stoned to death with no questions asked. Choosing to either forgive or justly punish a violation of God's Law was not an option under the law of Dt. 19:16-21.

Perhaps several simple questions will help clarify our thinking:

1. Is it essential that a magistrate and court enforce on individuals the justice of the laws of our land or should murders and false witnesses be allowed to go unpunished? The answer is obvious unless you deny the validity and righteousness of the law.

2. Is it impossible for a magistrate to either demand or force an individual to show grace and not protect himself against injustice? Again, the same answer is just as obvious unless you deny the true nature of both law and grace.

3. Do the answers to these two questions clearly point out the distinct and vital difference between what it means to be "under the law" as compared to being "under grace?" The answer to that is just as obvious to any honest and literal interpretation of the Sermon on the Mount and the rest of the New Testament Scriptures.

In other words, it is essential that Mt. 5:38 be the basis of justice upon which a magistrate settles disputes. In principle that is the law of our land today. When the court forces an individual to pay to fix a fender that he dented in an accident but refuses to make him pay for other things wrong with the car that were not caused by the accident, the magistrate is applying the principle of "eye for eye and tooth for tooth." He is saying, "The penalty must fit the crime (eye for eye), and the just penalty *must be paid*." Is the **main** purpose of this law to protect against *excessive* payment or is it to make sure that the fender is fixed and paid for by the man responsible for denting it?

It is just as essential that Mt. 5:39-42 should never be made the law of the land and be put into the hands of the magistrate. How would you like to live in a society where a judge could force you to give or loan to every individual that asked you? What would you say if you hit a man's 1975 car and slightly dented one fender and the magistrate told you that you had to buy the man a brand new Oldsmobile just because it was a "gracious" thing to do? You would rightly claim that his judgment was contrary to justice.

We would say the same thing to any civil judge that tried to make Christ's words in Mt. 5:39-42 be the basis of any of his decisions. A judge can only make judgments and demands based on the accepted law of the land. He cannot make demands that are based on grace. A judge may "suggest" a gracious act but he cannot demand and use the power of law to enforce it. The exact opposite is true of Christ. He can and does *demand*, in the sense of law, a "gracious response" from His disciples because they live "under grace." It is clear that this is the real difference between the legal covenant of Moses and the gracious covenant of Christ. The failure to see this radical contrast and vital difference will always cause a mixing of law and grace that distorts the doctrine of both justification and sanctification.

As Christians living under the gracious New Covenant, we gladly put our conscience under the obligation to obey the clear objective laws of the kingdom of Christ in Mt. 5-7. Christ not only has the right to make these new and higher laws, but He can also ground His demand on the fact of His death and not the threat of our death.

We simply must see that Christ is demanding of His disciples not only much more than Moses actually legislated, but also more than you can "logically deduce" from that legislation. The New Covenant embodies laws that the Old Covenant of law could never have embodied without contradicting itself. In some cases, our following Christ's new demands actually makes our behavior based on grace to be something that pure law could not even have *allowed* let alone *demanded!*

We may, as a Christian, forgive a false witness, but in Israel under the Law of Moses it would not have been allowed. A false witness violated God's covenant and *had to be punished* accordingly (Dt. 19:16-21). We may "pity" and show "grace" in the same situation where an Israelite was specifically forbidden to show pity and a judge was compelled to take "eye for eye." The vindication of justice and the honoring of God's law in judgment took precedence over everything else under the Law of Moses. This is one of the main differences between being "under a legal covenant" and being "under a gracious covenant."

We must keep on emphasizing that this is not to suggest that there was no grace or mercy under Moses' law. But it is to say that a *physical* nation under a *legal* covenant and a *spiritual* nation under a *gracious* covenant are two entirely different things. Moses and Israel is not Christ and the Church! The law in the hands of Moses as a covenant of life and death and functioning as a pedagogue in the conscience, and the indwelling Holy Spirit of adoption functioning as the new pedagogue in the renewed conscience of a New Covenant believer is not at all the same situation. It is the difference between the nature of rule by a sword and justice under a covenant of law and the nature of rule by the cross and mercy under a covenant of grace.

One modern commentator gives a clear and simple summation of Mt. 5:38-42. After covering the meaning of the three texts in the Old Testament Scriptures where the "eye for eye" law is mentioned, he concludes this way:

> . . . And most important of all, it must be remembered that the *Lex Tallionis* [Law of "eye for eye" or "tit for tat"] is by no means the whole of the Old Testament ethics. There are glimpses and even splendors of mercy in the Old Testament. "Thou shalt not avenge or bear any grudge against the children of thy people" (Leviticus 19:18). "If thine enemy be hungry, give him bread to eat; if he be thirsty, give him water to drink" (Proverbs 25:21). "Say not, I will do so to him as he hath done to me" Proverbs 24:29). "He giveth his cheek to the smiter; he is filled with reproach" (Lamentations 3:30).
>
> So, then, ancient ethics were based on the law of tit for tat. It is true that law was **a law of mercy;** it is true that it was a law for a **judge** and not for a **private individual;** it is true that there were **accents of mercy** at the same time. But Jesus **obliterated the very principle of that law,** because retaliation, however controlled and restricted, has **no place** in the Christian life.[20]

[13]Abraham's attitude and actions toward Lot are one example of this fact (Gen. 13:6-9). However, Abraham could not have been judged to have "broken God's law" if he had not acted as he did. Law and justice can demand honest and fair actions but they cannot demand *gracious* actions. *Likewise, law and justice cannot punish ungracious behavior.*

[14]Every "moral law" that God ever gave is a revelation of His holy character and that character never changes. However, every law does not *equally* reveal God's holy character. Christ's words in the Sermon on the Mount are a fuller and higher revelation of God's holy character than anything that preceded it, including the Ten Commandments. The holy character of God is identical in every age, but more and greater revelation reveals more of His holiness. The personal life and works of our Lord Jesus Christ are far more than just an example of "living out the Law of Moses." It surely does that, but it does far more. It reveals both God himself and His moral character in a way that makes the Ten Commandments appear as a dim outline or shadow.

[15]Greg L. Bahnsen, *Theonomy in Christian Ethics*, The Craig Press, pgs 63,90,119.

[16]Lloyd-Jones, Ibid, p 271

[17]I would not want anything I have said to keep anyone from buying Lloyd-Jones' book on the Sermon on the Mount. I can say without any reservation that I believe it is the finest commentary that has ever been written on that section of Scripture. If you do not have this book, **BUY IT IMMEDIATELY!**

[18]**Everything that God commands a person to do is "morally binding" on that individual at** *that time*. It was "morally wrong" for Adam to eat a piece of fruit from a particular tree simply because God told him not to do so. It was "morally right" for David to offer a lamb in sacrifice and it was not "morally wrong" for him to marry Bathesheba even though he already had several other wives.

[19]Lloyd-Jones, ibid, p 272,3

[20]William Barclay, *Gospel of Matthew, Vol. 1*, **Saint Andrew Press, p 163.**

★ ★ ★

FIVE

"Holy Hate for 'the Glory of God' "

Y *ou have heard that it hath been said, thou shalt love thy neighbor, and hate thy enemies.* **but I say unto you,** *love your enemies.* . . .

Mt. 5:43,44

There are few passages in the New Testament Scriptures that are as well known as this one, and there are also few passages that have been more misused than this one. The first question to ask is this: Did the Pharisees, and their teachers, *have any justification at all* for teaching that the Jews should "hate their enemies" or is this an open and shut case of national bigotry twisting and adding to the Word of God? Here is Pink's comments on this passage:

> The Pentateuch will be searched in vain for any precept which required the Israelites to entertain any malignity against their foes: thou shalt "hate thine enemies" was a **rabbinical invention** pure and simple.[21]

Before we look at the specific Old Testament passages that the Pharisees misused, let us ask a serious question. Have you ever known of a church or preacher that taught his congregation that it was their *"duty to Christ"* to treat people who left that particular local church as enemies of Christ and worthy of true *hatred?* We have personally heard that diatribe on more than one occasion, and the reasoning and use of Biblical texts for such an exhortation was *no better than that used by the Pharisees to justify their attitude of hatred of their enemies.* This is tragic but true.

It is ironical that the very same people who ridicule the Rabbinical distortion of Scriptures will themselves use *both* the same Scripture verses and the identical method of distortion to justify their own hatred of brethren that dared to question or disagree with the authority structure! History has witnessed some very ungodly behavior that was done under the guise of "love for God's truth." The perpetrators of the cruel deeds may have been sincere, but their hatred appeared to reveal the same attitude as that of the Jews in their treatment of those "dirty Gentiles?" The worst part of this tragic perversion of Scripture is that history is being repeated today. The rationale used by the Pharisees to justify their hatred of the Gentiles is the identical rationale being used by some church leaders today to justify their wrong attitude toward sincere brethren who have refused to "submit to the 'God-ordained' authority of the elders" in a local church.

The following application of "God's clear truth" is being used by "duly authorized servants of God" when someone leaves a local church:

    (1)   "These people have forsaken Christ's duly authorized Church which is the 'pillar and ground of the truth' (I Tim. 3:15)."

    (2)   "Christ loved the Church and gave Himself for it."

    (3)   "In leaving God's duly authorized Church, these people show that they hate the very thing that Christ loves the most."

    (4)   "The Psalmist said, 'I hate them, O Lord, that hate thee' (Ps. 139:21), and, 'I hate them with a perfect hatred' (Ps. 139:22). Since these people have proven their hatred of Christ (by leaving His church), it is our *duty to God* to hate these people with a *perfect hatred* because they have left Christ's Church which He loves above all else."

This is the word-for-word rationale used by churches with a cultic mentality for literally forcing their members to despise and shun anyone who dares to leave that particular congregation or group. The only reason these modern day "duly authorized" defenders of the "glory of God's Holy truth" have not run a sword through their enemies is only because they do not have the civil authority to do so!

Lloyd-Jones takes several pages in his commentary on the Sermon on the Mount to discuss how the Jews may have misconstrued God's command to kill all the inhabitants of Canaan as a command to "hate them as enemies." He also discusses the imprecatory Psalms where David "hated the enemies of God." In no way is Lloyd-Jones justifying the Pharisees, but he is attempting to state the case fairly. He emphasizes that both the Canaanite incident and the imprecatory Psalms are to be considered as national and judicial and in no way personal.[22] Lloyd-Jones is philosophically right, but at the same time, it seems unlikely that an individual could be "emotionally neutral" while carrying out the wholesale national slaughter of God's enemies. It would have been very difficult for an Israelite to convince either the Canaanite, or his own heart, that he really "loved his enemy" while killing the man and his family.

We have not found one single commentator that used the following passages when discussing the Rabbinical teaching of "hating your enemies:"

> *Thou shalt not seek their [Ammonites or Moabites] peace nor their prosperity all thy days for ever. Thou shalt not abhor an Edomite; for he is thy brother: Thou shalt not abhor an Egyptian; because thou wast a stranger in his land.*

Dt. 23:6,7.

Let us look at this sample passage in the Old Testament Scriptures and apply some of Thomas Watson's rules of interpreting commandments that we listed in chapter three. We will use his rules to extract, or deduce, the "good and necessary consequences" from the specific commandments in Dt. 23:6,7. It may help us to see whether the Jews had any reason at all to imagine that it was their duty to "hate their enemies." Let us restate, in abbreviated form, Watson's rules of interpreting commandments in Scripture:

Rule 2. More is intended than is spoken.
> (1) Where any duty is commanded, the contrary is forbidden.
> (2) Where any sin is forbidden, the contrary is commanded.

Rule 3. Where any sin is forbidden in the commandment, the occasion of it is also forbidden. Where murder is forbidden, envy and rash anger are forbidden, which may occasion it.

Rule 5. Where greater sins are forbidden, lesser sins are also forbidden.

Rule 7. A commandment forbids not only the acting of sin in our own persons, but being accessory to, or having any hand in, the sins of others.

Now what is the specific thing commanded in Dt. 23:6,7? There are two commandments and they both involve the treatment of certain kinds of people. The Jews were commanded to **not abhor** some people, and **not seek the peace or prosperity** of some other people.

First thing commanded: "Do not seek the peace or the prosperity of the Ammonite or Moabite." This was in retaliation for their treachery against Israel, vs 3,4.

Second thing commanded: "Do not abhor an Edomite or an Egyptian." This was because of relationship and gratitude vs. 7.

First of all, verses 6 and 7 specifically contrast two different attitudes and treatment of others on the basis of either retaliation or gratitude. Two different attitudes are set forth as opposites of each other. Let us apply Watson's rules to these commandments.

Rule 2 applied to the first thing commanded (*"Where any sin is forbidden, the contrary is commanded."*): What is the opposite of "seek the peace and prosperity?" The opposite of peace is war and the opposite of prosperity is poverty. The "good and necessary consequences" of Dt. 23:6,7, according to Watson's rules of interpreting commandments, clearly prove that it was Israel's duty to seek the destruction of the Edomites and Ammonites. There can be no other conclusion according to Watson's rule that any sin forbidden carries in it the duty to do the opposite. Is this not a true application of Watson's second rule of interpreting the commands of Scriptures? Would not Watson's rules literally make the Jew duty bound to hate the Ammonites and Moabites as enemies and constantly seek their destruction?

Rule 2 applied to the second thing commanded: What is the opposite of "abhor?" The opposite of abhor is love. In this specific context "abhor" is set in direct opposition to "seek peace and prosperity." The Jew was commanded to "love" some people, and if Watson's rules of interpreting commandments are correct, "to abhor," or hate, some other people.

Application: If Watson's rules are correct, it is our God given duty to "seek the peace and prosperity" (which means "love") of some men and to "abhor (which means 'hate') some other men." We must *not* hate the Edomites and Egyptians, but we *must hate* the Ammonites and the Moabites. We dare not "seek the peace and prosperity" of the Ammonites and Moabites, but must actively follow a course of action designed to destroy them. On the contrary, we must do all we can to "seek the peace and prosperity" of the Edomites and Egyptians.

Rule 3. "How can we consistently avoid any and every occasion that might possibly lead to an Edomite or Ammonite enjoying peace and prosperity?" We will let the reader work out a careful and studied approach in every detail of the "total shunning" process towards "God's enemies" who are under Elder discipline.

Rule 5. 'What should we include on the list of 'lesser' sins so as to think and act under all circumstances to be sure we do not in the least help the Edomite and Ammonite to have peace and prosperity. But to the contrary, we are making sure that he suffers the just consequences of his sin against God and His people"?

Rule 7. "What can we do to make sure that every person over whom we have any influence will also not seek the peace and prosperity of the Edomites and Ammonites, but instead, will also do the exact opposite and seek their destruction?"

Enough is enough. The point has been made. Now we know that the devotees of Covenant Theology are going to smile and say that we are caricaturing and misusing Thomas Watson. We also know that any honest and objective soul will clearly realize that the Jews had *more justification* for believing that God wanted them to "hate their *enemies*" than some of the Reformers and Puritans (Covenant Theologians to a man) had for killing *brethren in Christ* simply because some of those brethren dared to "re-baptize" believers and rejected the sacral sign (infant baptism) of the state church. It was the Covenant Theology of the Reformers and Puritans that led them to set up governments according to the Law of Moses. They patterned everything after the nation of Israel, especially as it pertained to the duty of the magistrate to punish all those who dissented from the doctrines or practices of the state church in power. This is an indisputable fact written in the book of history with the blood of the baptists, quakers, and others.

The case against the Puritans and Reformers for their atrocities is far more damaging than the case against the Pharisees. The Pharisees had only to distort a few Old Testament Scriptures, but the Puritans and Reformers not only had to distort those *very same Scriptures,* they also had to contradict both the clear commandments of the New Testament Scriptures that speak about loving the brethren and the whole tenor of Christ's clear teaching in the Sermon on the Mount.

It is impossible to read the history of the vain attempts by Covenant Theologians to make the "fine points of the law" to be the "chief instrument in a Christian's sanctification" without seeing a perfect parallel to both the attitude of the Pharisees and what has been written above. The places, faces and specific issues may be different, but the method of approach and disastrous results are identical. If the Pharisees interpreted Dt. 23:6,7 in exactly the same manner that Watson interpreted the Ten Commandments, they would have been more than justified in believing that God's Word literally "commanded" them hate to their enemies.

Most of us have seen church leaders with a cultic mentality exhibiting the same kind of attitudes that we condemn in the Pharisees. The worst part of the tragedy is not the attitude itself but the fact that it was motivated by the *identical* approach to the Word of God as that used by the Pharisees! Oh, that we could only learn to live and breathe under the freedom of the New Covenant! Oh, that the power of sovereign grace would grip our hearts and fill our souls with the love of Christ that we would not only love our *enemies,* but we would also be able to love our *brethren who disagree with our particular creed!*

If we would seriously compare Mt. 5:43-48 with the verses

in I John that make "love of the brethren" to be the practical test of assurance of salvation, then many great men in history and some at the present time would have a suspect salvation. The problem that produces such a situation is the very thing that we are discussing in this book. When we draw our whole system of conduct out of the Law of Moses, we will always fail to see Christ giving higher and more spiritual rules of conduct. We will become law centered instead of Christ centered. And when this happens we will automatically start acting more like God's sheriff than His shepherd. The present abuse of God's sheep by tyrannical Elders is far more than a personality or temperament problem. Its roots are a theological misunderstanding of the very subject that we are discussing in this book.

The Puritans and Reformers, in their own minds, were "sincerely obeying God's commandments" when they persecuted and even killed fellow Christians for rejecting the authorized creed. Those godly men were merely being consistent with the view of authority and law set forth in their Covenant Theology. Burning a witch was in no way the "aberration of a hard hearted tyrant." It was the "good and necessary consequence" of a wrong theology of the relationship between Moses and Christ.

As long as people insist that there can be no real change from the old legal covenant to the new gracious covenant, it will be impossible for them to see and feel the power of the new demands of Christ that are based entirely on pure grace. They must ultimately lock themselves into a legal mentality that cannot help but work itself out in a rigid, self-righteous, condemning attitude. We have heard men infected with this mentality ridicule and mock "love" in an angry screaming voice. Given the authority and opportunity, men with such an attitude and theology can very easily "punish heresy with death" and feel that God is "being glorified and His truth is being vindicated." It has happened before and it will happen again.

We are in no way suggesting that the Rabbinical fathers were even close to correct in making the Old Testament Scriptures teach that it was a duty to "hate your enemies." This is one of the clear instances in the Sermon on the Mount where Christ is showing the distortions of the Pharisees. We believe that Christ was literally accusing them of adding to the Word of God. However, if we are honest with history, we are forced to admit to at least two facts:

One: The Rabbinical leaders' method and logic in using the Old Testament Scriptures to justify their hatred of "God's enemies" (the Gentiles) was exactly like the method and logic that was often used by Rome, the Reformers and the Puritans to justify their hatred and persecution of sincere Christians who disagreed with the state church in power at the time. Tragically, the same thing can be said about some "duly authorized" church leaders today.

Two: According to Watson's rules of understanding God's commandments, "hating your enemies" was just as clearly a "good and necessary consequence" of some Old Testament texts as were many of the "good and necessary consequences" that were "deduced" by a consistent application of Covenant Theology and then used as the grounds to justify hatred and persecution. As already mentioned, the Pharisees were even more justified than the Covenant Theologians. While the Pharisees only had to distort the Old Testament Scriptures, Covenant Theologians have to misuse the *same texts* in the Old Testament Scriptures as well as contradict the *clear commandments in* the New Testament Scriptures. *The Pharisees hated the Gentiles and treated them as "God's enemies." The Reformers and Puritans hated and persecuted other Christians as "enemies of God."*

---

[21]A.W. Pink, Ibid. p. 129.

[22]See Lloyd-Jones, ibid, Vol 1, p 300.

SIX

Laws For Sinners and Laws For Saints

*It has been said, "Anyone who divorces his wife must give her a certificate of divorce." **But I tell you** that anyone who divorces his wife, except for marital unfaithfulness, causes her to become an adulteress, and anyone who marries the divorced woman commits adultery.*
Matthew 5:31,32.

The above verses clearly prove that Christ *changed and added* to the Law of Moses. It is impossible to study the subject of divorce in the Old Testament Scriptures and the New Testament Scriptures without seeing a clear difference. This does not constitute a contradiction in the sense that Moses was *wrong* and needed to be corrected. It does mean that Moses was perfectly correct *for that particular time and situation* because he was dealing with lost sinners on the basis of law. Under the New Covenant there are different rules simply because Christ is dealing with regenerate saints on the basis of grace. The foundation of the Church is a covenant of grace and not a covenant of law. But that does not mean that there are no "objective rules" under grace nor does it mean that there was no grace before Christ came.

Two things have been established so far. First, grace can and does, by its very nature, demand a higher morality than law could ever demand. Christ's rejection of "uncleanness" as a ground for

divorce, even though it was clearly allowed by the Law of Moses
(Dt. 24:1-4), is a further proof of this first fact. Christ literally
"changed the rules" on the subject of divorce because He changed
the covenant foundation from law to grace. Second, grace which
rules a believer's conscience can produce a kind of behavior that
transcends what the law cannot even *demand* let alone actually
produce. This is doubly true when the demands are given to true
believers as compared to their being given to unsaved rebels like
the Israelites.

Strangely enough, the clearest proof of this position comes
from the same people who vehemently disagree with what we
have just said. Pink's comments on Mt. 5:31,32 are an illustration:

> Moses had been indeed **divinely directed** to **allow di-
> vorce in cases of uncleanness**, for the **prevention of
> worse crimes. But that which had been no more
> than a temporary concession was changed by the
> Pharisees into a** *precept*[23] **and that so interpreted as
> to give license to the indulging of their evil and self-
> ish desires. . . .**

> Let us now consider a few details in Dt. 24:1-4. The first
> thing is the **kind** of statute there given. It was not a moral
> but a political or civil one[24] for the good ordering of the
> state. Among such laws were those of *tolerance or **per-
> mission, which did not approve** of **the evil things
> concerned,**[15] but only suffered them for the prevention
> of *greater evil—**as when the sea makes a breach into
> the land, if it cannot possibly be stopped, the best
> course is to make it as narrow as
> possible. . . . These laws** tolerated **what God** condem-
> ned, **and that for the** purpose **of preventing** greater
> evils.

When Pink gets to the point of telling us what Christ actually
did mean in His "*But I say unto you*" contrasts in Mt. 5-7, he
explains Christ's words this way:

> "But I say unto you, that whosoever shall put away his
> wife, saving for the cause of fornication, causes her to
> commit adultery: and whosoever shall marry her that is
> divorced committeth adultery" (verse 32). Here Christ

refutes the **corrupt interpretation** of the scribes and
Pharisees, and positively affirms that divorce is permis-
sible **only** in the case of that sin which in God's sight
disannuls the marriage covenant, and even then it is only
allowed and not commanded. . . . [26]

Let the reader take note that neither Dt. 24:1-4 nor anything
that Christ said suggests what Pink is saying. What is "positively"
affirmed in the two passages is the following:

1. Moses, in Dt. 24:1-4, allowed divorce for reasons *other than
adultery*.

2. Christ, in Mt. 5:31,32 and Mt. 19:1-9 rejected those same
reasons and allowed divorce *only on the ground of adultery*. The
Law of God given through Moses *positively allowed* what Christ
specifically rejected. The texts of Scripture are clear.

Lloyd-Jones takes basically the same approach as Pink. After
showing that it was God's original intention at creation (Gen.
2:24) for marriage to be "one wife for one man," Lloyd-Jones
raises the obvious objection to what he is stating:

"If that is so," asks someone, "how do you explain the
Law of Moses? If that is God's own view [The Creation
Ordinance] of marriage why did He allow divorce to take
place on the conditions which we have just considered?"
Our Lord again answered that question by saying that,
because of the hardness of their hearts, **God made a concession,** as it were. He did not **abrogate his original
law** with regard to marriage. No, He introduced a **temporary legislation** because of the **conditions then pre-
vailing.** [27]

We basically agree with much of what both Pink and Lloyd-
Jones have said because it fits very well into our view that:

1. a change of covenants brings a change in the laws;

2. the specific covenant laws under which any individual lives
is the basis upon which he is to order his life and by which he
will be judged by God;

3. Israel and the Church have a different canon of conduct,
or laws, on the subject of divorce because they live under different covenants. Israel lives under the Old Covenant of Moses
and the Church lives under the New Covenant of Christ.

What Pink and Lloyd-Jones are advocating is the right of Moses to make laws (they call them "temporary legislation") to govern moral behavior that are useful and necessary in "dispensations" characterized by certain sinful circumstances. We repeat, that fits into our view that a New Covenant with new laws has replaced an Old Covenant with its old laws. If however, that is not emphatically saying that a *different canon of conduct* governed the life of the nation of Israel than the canon of conduct that governs the Church, then two plus two does not equal four! It seems to us that Pink and Lloyd-Jones are adding to the very problem that they are trying to solve.

Pink has no right to believe what he said above. He is contradicting himself as long as he insists that Israel and the Church are *both under the identical canon of conduct!* It is simply impossible to fit Pink's statements into the frame work of Covenant Theology's view that Israel is the Church and therefore the same covenant and identical laws must govern both Israel the church. We simply cannot say that God instructed Moses to "allow" legitimate divorce for "uncleanness" in Israel, but Christ refused to accept the same "uncleanness" to be a legitimate grounds for divorce in the church, and then try to teach that Christ never changed the Law of Moses. That is simply not being honest with the stated facts in the case. Allowing Moses to make the concession concerning uncleanness even though it violates the revealed will of God as seen in the Creation Ordinance complicates Pink's problem even more. In the final analysis, Pink is saying that God can instruct Moses to give laws to govern Israel's conduct that Christ will not accept as laws to govern the Church simply because those laws are contrary to *the real law* of God according to Gen. 2:24. We will come back to this obvious contradiction later.

Let us be sure that we understand what Pink and Lloyd-Jones are saying, and then we will see if that is what Christ is really teaching. Here is a summary of their view:

One: Christ was showing that the Pharisees had "changed" a *concession* concerning divorce into a precept, and this somehow gave them the "license to the indulging of their evil and selfish desires." Christ was condemning the Pharisees for changing the Law of Moses and was not in any way contrasting His teaching with what Moses had actually said.

Two: God allowed, not commanded, divorce in Israel on the

grounds of "uncleanness." But "uncleanness" could not mean or include adultery since that was "punished by death."

Three: Divorce for uncleanness was purely a "concession" that was necessary at that time because of Israel's "hardness of heart" and the "chaotic conditions" that resulted from their attitude. God "allowed" easy divorce and polygamy (even though both were really adultery and a violation of the Seventh Commandment) but He did not "legitimate" it.

Four: The sole purpose of this particular law was to "narrow" the effects of sin and misery by condoning a clear breach of God's original moral law (one man and one wife as given in the Creation Ordinance) by legislation that would control to some degree an intolerable situation of the moment and protect women from the cruelty that could easily be expressed by Israel's hard-hearted men.

Five: The allowance of divorce for "uncleanness" was not meant to be a permanent part of God's law but was given only by Moses for that particular time and situation.

For the moment, let us assume that the texts of Scripture show that all of these statements are basically correct, even though in reality some of them contradict each other. The statements would still miss the point under discussion. They never touch the heart of the problem in trying to understand Christ's contrasts in the Sermon on the Mount. In fact, the more true the statements are, the more difficulty you have fitting them into Pink's own theology. This view makes the problem *worse.* The cure is worse than the disease. Moses, in Dt. 24:1-4, is now contradicting himself and the real Law of God concerning marriage that he, Moses himself, recorded in Gen. 2:24. God is now instructing Moses to give this contradictory legislation on "dispensational" grounds due to Israel's "hardness of heart." It seems strange to hear people that oppose anything that even suggests a "dispensational" approach to Scripture taking the foregoing position on these particular verses.

The whole point of Mt. 19:1-9 is this: Christ very emphatically states that the Law of Moses in Dt. 24:1-4 legislated and allowed certain moral conduct for an Israelite that could not possibly be tolerated under the New Covenant in the life of a Christian today! Now this point is as clear as crystal. It does not in the least matter *why* Moses made the concession or why Christ changed the rules and rejected the concession. The only question at the moment is this: *Did Christ change the Law of Moses concerning marriage and divorce?* A comparison of Dt. 24:1-4 and 5:31,32 forces us to answer, "Yes." And the new Lawgiver had every right to make the change.

It is impossible to be honest with words and deny that the Law of Moses, given by God, *allowed* what Christ specifically *rejected*. It is likewise not possible to accept the fact that Christ changed one of the laws that Moses gave and also hold on to a "one covenant, one church, and one canon of conduct for all ages" view. The moment we take Christ's words of contrast seriously we see that He is contrasting His teaching with the Law of Moses in Dt. 24:1-4 and not with the Pharisees supposed distortion of that law. Moses, *not the Pharisees*, wrote the legislation in Dt. 24:1-4 allowing divorce for uncleanness, and it that specific law that Christ refuses to allow in the Church. The situation that necessitated the law that Moses gave in no way changes the *fact* that he *gave the law*. However, understanding *why* Christ changed the Law of Moses on this point greatly strengthens our case even further.

Why would God instruct Moses to write a law for Israel's moral conduct in the marriage relationship that Christ would never instruct an Apostle to write for the moral conduct of a Christian under the New Covenant? The answer to that question lies in understanding the difference between a covenant of law designed specifically for sinners and a covenant of grace made only with saints.

Let us first look at the specific Law of Moses that Christ rejected and changed:

> *When a man hath taken a wife, and married her, and it come to pass that she find no favor in his eyes, because he hath found some uncleanness: then let him write her a bill of divorcement, and give it in her hand, and send her out of his house. And when she is departed out of his house, she may go and be another man's wife. And if the latter husband hate her, and write her a bill of divorcement, and giveth it in her hand, and sendeth her out of his house; of if the latter husband die, which took her to be his wife; Her former husband, which sent her away, may not take her again to be his wife, after*

*that she is defiled; for that is abomination before the
Lord: and thou shalt not cause the land to sin, which
the Lord thy God giveth thee for an inheritance.*

Dt. 24:1-4.

First of all, as both Lloyd-Jones and Pink emphasize, the
"uncleanness" cannot be the sin of adultery. This immediately
shows the total change and difference between the Law of Moses
and the law of Christ on the subject of divorce. It would have
been impossible for Moses to legislate the new law of Christ that
allows divorce only for adultery without clearly contradicting
himself. And it was just as impossible for Christ to accept the Law
of Moses concerning divorce for "uncleanness" as the rule for
the Church without contradicting the very nature and power of
grace.

This one clear change is all we need to prove the position
that Christ gave new and higher laws in the Sermon on the
Mount than Moses gave in the Old Covenant. All we have to
prove to establish this basic thesis is that Christ clearly gave
a different law for the Church on the subject of divorce and
polygamy than Moses gave to Israel. These are Biblical facts
regardless of what the reasons were for the change. Actually
Christ did more than give a new law, He also did away with
the death penalty for adultery. Moses could have done neither
of these things without contradicting himself and the laws God
gave through him.

The second thing to note is *the circumstances under which
the "concession" of Dt. 24:1-4 was given in the first place.* Our
Lord tells us in Mt. 19:1-9 that Moses, by inspiration, gave a law
that tolerated what was clearly contrary to God's original purpose for Adam and Eve at Creation. It seems obvious from Christ's
words that the purpose of the law in Dt. 24:1-4 was to control
the effects of Israel's "hardness of heart." We all agree so far.
However, at this point some wrong assumptions are made. We
must start with the facts in the text itself before we start
"deducing" any "good and necessary consequences" to fit into
our theological system.

At no point in either Mt. 5:31,32 or in Mt. 19:1-9, is Christ
attacking or correcting a rabbinical distortion of Dt. 24:1-4 and
giving us the "true spiritual meaning" of what Moses meant in
these verses. In order to do this Christ would have had to tell

us exactly what Moses meant by "uncleanness." Christ is not merely *interpreting* Scripture, He is giving us *new* Scriptures. He is changing the Law of Moses from allowing divorce for "uncleanness" to allowing divorce *only for adultery.* Mt. 19:1-9 has nothing whatever to do with the Pharisaical interpretation or application of Dt. 24:1-4. Christ is dealing with Israel's hardness of heart that caused Moses to give the "concession" concerning uncleanness in the first place. It is not the *abuse* of Dt. 24:1-4, but the very *need* of such a law that Christ is condemning.

Christ is **not** saying to the Pharisees, "I will not tolerate your distortion of the Law of Moses," but rather He is saying, "I will not tolerate in My kingdom the legislation that Moses gave because of the hardness of heart of your rebellious fathers." It is impossible to have Christ giving us the "true exposition of the Law of Moses" in these particular passages (Mt. 5:31,32; Mt. 19:1-9). Our Lord is not settling the argument between the liberal and conservative Pharisees by telling us what Moses really meant by "uncleanness" in Dt. 24:1-4. Christ is saying, "The Law of Moses in Dt. 24:1-4 that allowed uncleanness as a ground of divorce is no longer accepted as part of the new canon of conduct for the church." *Christ literally changed the Law of Moses on the subject of divorce!* The texts can mean nothing else. We simply cannot make this passage teach that Christ is only reinforcing and rubber stamping the Law of Moses on the subject of divorce. Such a view misses the whole point.

It is essential that we see the radical difference between the two groups of people for whom the two different laws (Dt. 24:1-4 and Mt. 19:1-9), or canons of conduct, concerning divorce were given. It is this fact that gave us our chapter title "Laws for SINNERS and Laws for SAINTS." The laws of Christ in the kingdom of grace were not given to control the behavior of "hard hearted" sinners as in the case of the Law of Moses. Christ's law is given to regenerate saints who have a desire to obey and please God. Covenant Theology cannot grasp what has just been said because it views Israel as the Church, or "God's redeemed people under the Covenant of Grace."[28] They cannot believe that Israel was under a conditional legal covenant at Sinai. This simply will not fit into the system.

It is impossible for the situation that occasioned the Law of Moses concerning "uncleanness" to exist in Christ's Church under the rule of grace. Under the New Covenant, God's people, without a single exception, are **all** *regenerated saints with new hearts* (Heb. 8:10,11)! There are no "hard-hearted" sinners in the Body of Christ! The situation described in Mt. 19:8 that existed in Israel cannot possibly exist in the Church. It would deny both the reality and the power of the grace of God. It would turn salvation *from* sin into salvation *in* sin (Mt. 1:21).

The third thing we must discuss under this point is the use of *"Creation Ordinances"* as the *"real, unchanging Law of God"* that have a higher authority than the Law of Moses. Covenant Theology builds a complete system of morality and ethics on revelation given prior to the fall. These laws, called "Creation Ordinances," are considered to be the *real* revealed will of God to which all men are always subject. They are supposed to be written on man's heart and therefore need no special revelation from God in order to be known. The Creation Ordinances thus become the *real* unchanging moral Law of God for all time regardless of what any later revelation may or may not say.

This concept of "Creation Ordinances" creates some very difficult problems. In the case we are discussing, it means that the later revelation given by Moses in Dt. 24:1-4, under God's direction, was nonetheless in direct opposition to the Creation Ordinance given in Gen. 2:24 concerning marriage. This is the thesis of Professor John Murray in his book entitled *"Principles of Conduct."* The stated purpose of that book is to prove that both easy divorce and polygamy were just as sinful, even though not punished, in the Old Testament as in the New. The practice of polygamy was just as sinful for David as it would be for a Christian today. David literally broke the Seventh Commandment and lived most of his life in multiple adultery according to this view. God simply "overlooked" his sin and did not punish it even though David had every reason (because of the Creation Ordinance) to know that he was committing adultery.

There are several key problems which makes Murray's view impossible. Only a scholastic theologian could ever even pretend to figure out what the "real moral law of God" is. The ordinary Christian (as well as the Israelites to whom it was written) would read Dt. 24:1-4, where divorce is allowed for reasons other than adultery, and assume that those words were actually part of the "moral law" given to Israel to govern their life. However, Professor Murray, tediously arguing the position of Covenant Theology, informs us that the ordinary man would be totally wrong. Here is Murray's statement:

> The only thesis that appears to me to be compatible with these data is that polygamy and divorce (for light cause) were **permitted or tolerated** under the Old Testament, tolerated in such a way that **regulatory provisions were enacted** to prevent some of the grosser evils and abuses attendant upon them, and tolerated in the sense that they were not openly condemned and censured with civil and ecclesiastical penalties, but that nevertheless they were **not legitimated.**[29] That is to say, these practices were **basically wrong;** they were violations of a **creation ordinance,** even of an ordinance which had been revealed to man at the beginning. Therefore they were **inconsistent with the standards** and criteria of holy living which had been **established by God at the beginning.** They were really contrary to the **revealed will of God** and rested under His judgment.[30]

Professor Murray immediately acknowledges the obvious question raised by his own statement:

> The insistent question immediately arises: How could this be? How could God allow his people, in some cases the most eminent of Old Testament saints, to practice what was a **violation** of His **perceptive will?** It is a difficult question.[31]

It is a difficult question indeed. How can godly people be allowed to live in adultery and God appear to approve of the situation? We cannot agree with Professor Murray's answer to his own difficult question. But we are grateful that he himself had the courage to raise the question. It makes it impossible to accuse us of caricature. Professor Murray is one of the most honest writers that we have ever read. He does not duck the hard questions that his own system raises. Very few writers will ever admit to the serious problems they must honestly answer in order to be consistent with their position.

Professor Murray's book, *Principles of Conduct*, was the

"final straw" that led us out of classical Covenant Theology. His answers to the difficult questions confronting his own Covenant Theology view of law were by far the best answers ever given. If Murray's answers are not adequate, and they definitely are not, then there simply are no answers and the whole view of law demanded by that system is without Biblical foundation.[32]

What is the basic problem that Professor Murray is trying to resolve? He is dealing with the same problem that we have been dealing with in this book except he is giving a different answer. Professor Murray is trying to prove that Christ cannot change the Law of Moses that was given to Israel as a canon of conduct. Since he assumes there is only one covenant, there can only be one unchanging moral law for the one unified church of God in all ages. Since Israel is the Church in the Old Testament according to Covenant Theology, then it logically, and necessarily, follows that Old Testament Israel and the Church today must be under the same law, or canon of conduct. Murray's theology must prove that point or else its basic presupposition concerning law and grace is destroyed. It *had to be* just as sinful for David to practice polygamy as it would be for a Christian today or else the foundation of Covenant Theology is destroyed. Murray acknowledged and faced this fact and his book *Principles of Conduct* is his earnest attempt to solve that very problem. He himself states the major problems to his own theology in the following facts:

1.   "It is a patent fact" that Abraham and David's polygamy would be recognized and condemned as adultery in the church today.

2.   Yet the Old Testament Scripture gives no evidence whatever that either Abraham or David felt the least bit guilty for their polygamy.

3.   It is clear that God did not punish Old Testament believers for either the easy divorce of Dt. 24:1-4 or polygamy.

4.   Moses gave clear laws (by inspiration) that were "sanctioned and approved by God" and clearly "recognized as regulative" for *that period of time and circumstances,* even though those very laws clearly contradicted the "perceptive will of God" as seen in God's Creation Ordinance in Gen. 2:24 concerning marriage.

5. God both "allowed" and inspired Moses to give "laws
    to regulate" easy divorce for uncleanness (Dt. 24:1-4)
    and other laws to govern polygamy (Ex. 21:10,11), but
    did not "legitimate" either set of laws. The practices
    regulated were sinful even though they were
    "tolerated" by the laws given.
6. These laws actually tolerated the sin of adultery and did
    not punish it even though those who practiced it were
    responsible to God to know that such behavior was a
    clear breach of the Seventh Commandment as seen in
    the light of the Creation Ordinance of Gen. 2:24.[33]

The first time we read these problems as Murray set them forth
in his book, our reaction was to say, "Professor Murray must have
some very strong answers to the problems that he has raised or
he would not have admitted them so openly." Every one does
not agree that Murray's answers to the difficult questions that he
himself raised are correct. Some of us feel that Murray's case is
extremely weak even though we admire his honesty. What Murray is saying is this: God's revealed, or perceptive, will (Creation
Ordinance) is different from, and opposed to, the "canons of behavior" that were given to Moses in Dt. 24:1-4 even though those
very laws of Moses were "**recognized as regulative**" in the Old
Testament period. The Scriptures nowhere agree with such a
view. These conclusions were first arrived at by logic and then
"read back into" the Scripture as "theological truth." Murray's
view point was dictated as a "good and necessary consequence"
of his Covenant Theology. In reality, Murray must assume as a
fact, and then use as proof, the very point that he is trying to
establish.

Another problem with the position under discussion concerning Creation Ordinances is that it ignores the situation created
by the entrance of sin into the world as well as the stated purpose for which the law, as a legal covenant, was given at Mt. Sinai.
The position assumes that Abraham, Moses, and David were all
responsible to understand and apply Gen. 2:24 exactly as Christ
did in Mt. 19:4,5. If this were true, it would have been literally
impossible for Moses to give the law of Dt. 24:1-4 in the first
place. Moses would have been knowingly and deliberately contradicting what he knew was God's unchanging "perceptive will."
After all, Moses was the one who wrote Gen. 2:24! How could

Moses also write Dt. 24:1-4 if he knew that he was clearly contradicting Gen. 2:24? This dilemma cannot be escaped. There is no middle ground. It is either one way or the other.

Professor Murray is forced to declare that Moses was "allowed" to give a divorce law for "uncleanness" that was a clear contradiction of the Creation Ordinance which is the *real* Law of God. Was the law given in Dt. 24:1-24 part of the "Law of *God*" or was it only the "Law of *Moses*"? Does Moses have the authority to write laws for Israel that are "approved and sanctioned by God" but are still not really the "the *Law of God*"? Again, Professor Murray is both clear and emphatic:

> It is quite obvious that this statement of the case poses several questions. And **the most basic of these is the question:** Is there in the sense defined, a biblical ethic? Is there one coherent and consistent ethic set forth in the Bible? Is there not diversity in the Bible and diversity of a kind that embraces antithetical elements? Are there not in the Bible canons of conduct that are contrary to one another? To be specific: Is there not an antithesis between the **canons of conduct sanctioned and approved of God in the Old Testament and those sanctioned and approved of God** in the New in respect of certain central features of human behavior? It is a patent fact that the behavior of the most illustrious of Old Testament believers was characterized by practices which are clearly contradictory of the elementary demands of the New Testament ethic, Monogamy is surely a principle of the Christian ethic. Old Testament saints practiced polygamy. In like manner, under the Old Testament, divorce was practiced on grounds which could not be tolerated in terms of the explicit provisions of the New Testament revelation. And polygamy and divorce were practiced without overt disapprobation in terms of the **canons of behavior** which were **regulative** in the Old Testament period.[34]

Professor Murray must answer his question concerning the problem of two different canons of conduct with an emphatic "no." He must, and does, insist that there can only be one "canon of conduct" simply because his theology cannot allow any change in God's "one unchanging moral law." In other words:

1. God clearly gave, through Moses, a "canon of behavior" that "allowed" divorce for uncleanness (Dt. 24:1-4) and also gave specific rules for a polygamous marriage that forced a man to sleep with both, or all, of his wives (Ex. 21:10,11);

2. both the laws for easy divorce and polygamy were clearly "recognized as regulative" in the "canons of behavior" that governed the moral life of Israel;

3. However, despite these facts, those very laws were still contrary to the "perceptive will of God" as seen in the Creation Ordinance and therefore rested under the judgment of God even though ignored and unpunished by God;

4. and finally, both Moses and Israel were responsible to know and believe this last fact because it had been clearly revealed in the Creation Ordinance as God's unchanging moral law.

The final problem with making Creation Ordinances to be the "real law of God" to which everything else in Scripture must be compared is that it effectively renders all of the Scripture written after the fall to be basically "secondary" in the area of morality. In this view, all we need to do is apply correct logic to the Creation Ordinances and all of the problems of morality are automatically resolved. Nothing can be considered as absolute in ethics or morality unless it has its roots in, and gets its sanction from, a Creation Ordinance. Progressive revelation cannot in anyway change or add to the will of God as revealed in Creation ordinances. Later revelation can only clarify, explain, and reinforce the original and permanent law of God revealed in those ordinances.

In reality, when you think this through, this position denies the very principle that it is trying to defend, namely, that the laws of Christ in the Sermon on the Mount are the *true and spiritual* interpretation of the Law of Moses and in no sense a contrast. This idea is totally destroyed if Moses himself gave Israel laws that contradict Gen. 2:24. This is a classic "catch 22" situation. The Sermon on the Mount has now become, not the true interpretation of the *Law of Moses*, but the true interpretation of the

Creation Ordinance of Gen. 2:24. And worse, Christ appeals to the Creation Ordinance for the specific purpose of showing that the Law of Moses was *wrong*! It is a hollow victory that keeps Christ from contradicting Moses at the expense of having Moses contradict a Creation Ordinance!

It might be well to raise a few problems that Professor Murray did *not* raise that could easily lead to a denial of the inspiration of the Bible. If Dt. 24:1-4 is part of the Law of God that was given by God to Israel, then how can it contradict a Creation Ordinance (the *real* Law of God) without pitting the Law of God against the Law of God?

If it is objected that this is exactly what Christ did in Mt. 19:1-9 when He appealed to Gen. 2:24, then the argument would prove too much. It would prove that Christ was clearly *reproving and contradicting* Moses as being wrong in Dt. 24:1-4! This argument would totally destroy the very thing that the position is seeking to prove, namely, that Christ never in any way contradicts Moses. Christ would be flat out accusing Moses of knowingly contradicting God's revealed will as seen in the Creation Ordinance of Gen. 2:24 if Murray's application of Mt. 19:4,5 is correct.

It seems much better to view Christ as having authority to use a so called "Creation Ordinance" (or any other Scripture) as a proof text in a manner that we dare not. Does what Christ did with Genesis 2:24 give us the authority to arbitrarily use pre-fall revelation to construct our own system of ethics. Can we by logic alone, with no New Testament corroboration at all, discover in Gen. 1-2, the "real Law of God" for all people in all ages irrespective of the entrance of sin or any later revelation? We think not.

Regardless of which approach is taken in understanding Dt. 24:1-4 and Mt. 19:1-9, it is impossible to maintain that the canon of conduct for Israel and the Church is the same canon with no changes. Moses allowed divorce on the grounds of "uncleanness" and Christ refused to allow divorce on the same grounds. One thing is certain, the law that God gave to Israel is totally different than the law that Christ gave the Church on the subject of divorce and polygamy. We do not believe it is possible to deny this obvious Biblical fact. There is no problem with either the laws or the passages of Scripture when we see that there has been a change of covenants and we allow the specific covenant under which any individual lives to be the "Law of God" to that individual.

In order to keep Christ from in any way adding to or changing the Law of Moses. Professor Murray allows Moses to change the *real* Law of God as seen in the Creation Ordinance that condemns both divorce and polygamy? Simply stated, Professor Murray's Covenant Theology is telling us that Christ may not in any way change the canon of conduct given by Moses, but Moses may, because of Israel's hardness of heart, change the canon of conduct given by God in Creation Ordinances prior to the Fall!

If Professor Murray is correct in accusing Moses of giving a law that violated the Creation Ordinance of marriage, then did not Paul, in I Cor. 7:12-16, go against both Gen. 2:24 and Mt. 19:1-9 by adding *yet another ground for divorce*. We realize that some people do not believe that Paul allowed divorce and remarriage in this passage. However, Professor Murray's position is clearly set forth in his own book on divorce where his position proves that the Apostle Paul went beyond the Creation Ordinance, the Law of Moses, and the teaching of Christ by giving the additional ground for divorce.

Would it not be better to see that Christ, in Mt. 19:1-9, is doing exactly what Paul is doing in I Cor. 7? We have no trouble seeing that Paul gave new truth that neither the Creation Ordinance or Christ's interpretation of it in Mt. 19:1-19 could anticipate. Paul is covering a situation not covered by either Moses or Christ. Likewise, Moses covered a situation that cannot exist in the Church, and Christ gave new laws covering a situation that did not exist in the time of Moses. We must not strangle progressive revelation of new and higher moral truth just to hang on to a theory of "one covenant with two administrations" that has no textual basis in Scripture.

One last thought before we leave this point. Can we really use Israel's "hardness of heart" as the sole justification for easy divorce and polygamy under the Old Covenant? Can we honestly say, "They were actually breaking God's *real law* as found in a Creation Ordinance and therefore they were guilty in God's sight of violating the true meaning of the Seventh Commandment, but God simply chose to overlook their sin and not punish it?" Such a view actually allows Moses to give legislation that made certain behavior" legally acceptable" even though that behavior was "morally wrong."[35] Apart from the fact that such a view (allowing the sin of adultery and making laws to control its effects) appears to be nothing less than "shall we sin that grace may abound," or "is it right to do wrong if the goal is good," there is the greater problem of trying to know what the *real Law of God* is to which we are subject and by which we will be judged.

We have repeatedly pointed out that both Covenant Theology and Dispensationalism have a defective view of Israel's status before God. It is this fact that forces Covenant Theology to approach Mt. 5:31,32 in the manner in which it does. It is a classic example of theology dictating what a text *has to mean* instead of letting the text say what it means. On the one hand, Covenant Theology will insist that the nation of Israel cannot be put under a legal covenant at Mt. Sinai because it is the Church, or the "redeemed people of God" under the "everlasting covenant of grace," and it is impossible to put the "redeemed Church" under a legal covenant. On the other hand, when it must find a way to justify Moses in giving laws to the "redeemed church" that clearly contradict a Creation Ordinance (by allowing divorce on the grounds of "uncleanness"), Covenant Theology then insists that the same "redeemed church members" are such "hard hearted sinners" that God Himself was forced to allow them to practice the sin adultery as the only means available to bring order into a chaotic situation. Amazing!

How can we possibly believe that: (1) the people at Mt. Sinai were so hard hearted that their sin created a moral situation so chaotic that special legislation had to be given that condoned the actual sin of adultery as the only means available to avoid worse sin, and also at the same time believe that, (2) those same hard hearted sinners were "God's redeemed Church under a covenant of grace?" And if we can somehow merge these two opposites, how do we, (3) explain that a man "after God's own heart" who "meditated in the Law of God day and night" practiced multiple polygamy without any pangs of conscience? We cannot possibly lump godly David into the same group of "hard hearted" sinners that Jesus was talking about in Mt. 19:1-9. Yet this is the very thing that Covenant Theology is forced to do.

If Covenant Theology is correct and David's polygamy was really adultery under the Old Covenant, we can no more excuse his sin on the basis of "hardness of heart" than we could excuse a Christian doing the same thing today. Surely no one cannot honestly believe that God allowed Abraham and David to practice, for their entire life time, adulterous polygamy without punishment on the grounds that they were "hard hearted sinners" living in "chaotic times." The problem of polygamy cannot be solved by turning David and Abraham into ungodly "hard hearted sinners." It can only be solved by seeing a change of covenants that sets a new and higher canon of conduct for the Church.

Godly David was not breaking the Seventh Commandment by living with more than one wife simply because the Mosaic covenant, or canon of conduct, under which David lived, clearly did not consider polygamy a sin. How could David have written Psalm 1 while living in multiple adultery? How could he, (1) have the same Holy Spirit indwelling and guiding him that believers have today, and (2) mediate day and night in the same code of "moral law" that has been given to us, and (3) yet not feel the least bit guilty for having multiple wives and thereby continually commit multiple adultery? A believer could not do the same thing today without feeling guilty before God because he meditates in a higher law. The same situation would be considered a horrible sin today only because we live under a New Covenant that lays down a higher canon of conduct for Christians than the canon of conduct laid down for an Israelite. The new canon makes polygamy to be a sin.

It seems to us that both Lloyd-Jones and Pink unknowingly prove the basic thesis of this book. The Law of Moses was absolutely essential for *that time*, for *those* people, and for *that situation* simply because the Israelites were hard hearted unregenerate rebels that needed a covenant of law to both convict them of their unbelief and control their rebellious hard hearts. The Body of Christ is NOT made up of hard hearted unregenerate sinners. Every member of the Church is regenerate and has a new heart (Jer. 31:33). All of the members of Christ's body not only have God's true law written on their hearts, they also, without exception, have the indwelling Holy Spirit of God as their *personal Pedagogue* to teach and direct them.

It would be ridiculous even to suggest that the Apostles would ever be instructed by Christ to give legislation to govern the conduct of His Church that allowed one kind of sin as the only means of controlling worse sin, especially if it involved a commandment as clear as "Thou shalt not commit adultery." Neither the legislation in Dt. 24:1-4 itself, nor the *reason or situation that occasioned the legislation being given* in the first place, are possible under the New Covenant in the life of the Church. The power of the grace of God makes both of those things impossible today (Titus 2:11,12).

This whole subject is as clear as crystal the moment we see that Christ established a New Covenant that replaces the Old Covenant, and that the New Covenant brings with it new and higher laws of conduct that are based entirely on grace. These new laws are just as objective as any law under the Old Covenant. These objective commands can demand a kind of behavior that Moses could never demand simply because these new laws are based on the truth and power of grace. These new demands are given to true believers and not to a nation of lost rebels. We must not confuse a *physical redemption from Egypt with a spiritual redemption* from sin.

---

[23]God's allowance of divorce for "uncleanness" may have been a "temporary concession" in God's *purposes*, but it was a **divine precept** to Israel or else it was not really part of "the Law of Moses" inspired and given by God.

[24]When you consider this law to be part of the "Law of God" to His covenant nation, and remember that it is dealing with a subject as intimate and moral as marriage, then Pink's statement is incorrect and a cop-out. The view we are taking in this book could make Pink's statement, but Pink is contradicting himself. His Covenant Theology will not allow him to separate the theocracy of Israel and the Church as the Body of Christ in respect to morality.

[25]In this case, "the evil things concerned" is no less that the sin of adultery, or breaking of the Seventh Commandment, according to Pink's application of the Creation Ordinance concerning marriage. What could possibly be considered a "greater evil in God's sight" than breaking one of the commandments written on the Tablets of the Covenant (Ex. 34:27,28)?

[26]Ibid, p 93.

[27]Lloyd-Jones, Ibid, p. 258.

[28]One of the basic errors of both Dispensationalism and Covenant Theology is their view of the Church, especially in its relationship to the nation Israel. We have worked this out in more detail in a forth coming book entitled *The Four Seeds of Abraham*. This book will be available from *Crowne Publications*, PO Box 699, Southbridge, Mass., 01550. It examines the basic presuppositions of both Dispensationalism and Covenant Theology as they relate to the "promise of God to Abraham and his seed."

[29]How can anyone read II Sam. 12:24,25 and say God "tolerated" but did not "approve" of both David's polygamous marriage to Bathsheba and the birth

of Solomon resulting from that marriage. Professor Murray must insist that Solomon's birth was just as much under God's wrath as the child that had just died since polygamy was adultery according to the clearly "revealed will of God" in the creation ordinance. God simply chose to "tolerate" and not punish the second instance of adultery as He did the first.

[30]From *Principles of Conduct*, by John Murray, Eerdmans, P. 16

[31]Ibid, p 16

[31]We have developed this point in more detail in a book entitled "*The Tablets of Stone*." It is available from *Crowne Publishers, Inc.*, P.O. Box 688, Southbridge, Mass., 01550.

[33]See *Principles of Conduct*, by John Murray, Erdmans, pgs 14-17.

[34]Ibid, p 14

[35]As already noted, this is the view taken by Professor Murray in *Principles of Conduct* (see pp 14-17).

★ ★ ★

SEVEN

Application and Implications

Nothing in this book is contrary to either the texts of Scripture under discussion or anything else in the rest of the Word of God. The approach taken has set forth both the Old Testament Scriptures and Christ's statements in the Sermon on the Mount in their contexts and at face value. The rest of the New Testament Scriptures certainly support a clear contrast between Israel being "under the law" and the Church being "under grace."[36] The only things contradicted in this book are the dictums of some theological systems.

We are **not** discussing whether a Christian's rule of life is governed by "objective truth or subjective love." We wholeheartedly agree that a Christian is not in any sense "lawless." Anyone who even suggests that we are pitting love against law and leaving Christians with only "subjective feelings" to govern their life is being deliberately dishonest. The question is **not** "objective law versus subjective love" as the rule to govern our life as Christians. We all agree that a believer's rule of life is *clear objective laws or commandments.* The heart of the issue is *where* the New Testament believer finds the **full** and **final** objective laws that are to govern his life and attitudes. The real question is this:

"Are the Ten Commandments **as written on the tables of stone in Exodus twenty** the highest standard

of moral conduct that was ever given, or is the teaching
of Christ in the Sermon on the Mount and in Holy Spirit
inspired Epistles an **even higher standard** of moral conduct?''

This is the real issue: Is the teaching and authority of Christ
merely equal to Moses or does He go beyond Moses and make
higher demands that cannot be found in the Law of Moses? Do
both the Sermon on the Mount and the New Testament Epistles
contain ethical and spiritual demands that go beyond anything
found in the Old Covenant law? Do, or do not, both our Lord
Jesus Christ and His Apostles insist that the New Covenant brings
with it a new and higher set of objective laws and demands? **The
greater and final authority of our Lord Jesus Christ as the
new and final Lawgiver is the heart of the issue!** Who is
really the "big man on campus" in the conscience of a child of
God living under the New Covenant—Moses or Christ? That is
the one vital question!

In making these statements, we are not in any way demeaning Moses. We are saying that a New Lawgiver has superceded
and gone far beyond what Moses and the law could ever do. We
refuse to belittle Moses in order to establish Christ. However, we
also refuse to demean Christ by making Him to be merely an equal
authority with Moses. We do not believe that Christ came merely
to interpret and rubber stamp Moses. Christ has given us new laws
that are based entirely on grace. Christ is the New Lawgiver over
the true house of God.

A correct understanding of the Sermon on the Mount must
at least establish the following things:

One: Christ is making new and higher demands on New
Covenant believers that cannot be found in the Old Covenant laws
that governed Israel. There is a new canon of conduct for the
Church.

Two: These new demands of Christ grow out of the reality
of the New Covenant being rooted in pure grace, and, although
the New Covenant in no way demeans or contradicts Moses and
the law, its demands go far beyond Moses.

Three: Christ is giving us more than just a correct interpretation of Moses. As "that *Prophet*" Who replaces Moses (Acts
3:22,23) as the new and greater Law Giver, Christ gave new and
higher laws for the kingdom of grace. In the Sermon on the

Mount, Christ is literally contrasting a way of living under a covenant of law and a way of living under a covenant of grace. He is also showing why the latter is so superior to the former even though both were given by the same God.

Four: Christ is not implying that Moses was in any way wrong or that the Old Covenant law was either cruel or inhumane. He is showing that *both* a rule by a legal covenant and a rule by a gracious covenant are both "just, holy, and good." However, one is superior to the other because it is based on "better promises" (Heb. 8:6). Both covenants have the *same goal,* but they function differently. The Old Covenant was given to "hard hearted sinners" as a "ministry of death" (II Cor. 3:7; Rom. 7:10) and preached condemnation to the conscience. In contrast, the New Covenant is given to saints having a new heart as a ministry of life (II Cor. 3:9) that sets the conscience free from condemnation (Heb. 10:16-18; Rom. 8:1,2).

Five: The Law of Moses was given to a *physical nation of unregenerate sinners,* but the Law of Christ is given to a *spiritual nation of regenerate saints.* Both the purpose and the nature of the objective laws are different in each case. In one case, the designed purpose of the Law of Moses is conviction of sin in the conscience of sinners that leads to justification by faith. In the other case, the purpose of the Law of Christ is to furnish the renewed mind of saints with truth that leads to a more sanctified life.

Six: The Sermon on the Mount clearly shows that grace can and does make legitimate demands that law can never make. The Church can demand a certain behavior from its members that Moses could never demand of an Israelite. The Church is given objective laws that demand behavior that is based entirely on grace and the power of the indwelling Spirit. Moses could neither demand that kind of behavior nor punish its absence by the sword.

There is one last observation. If what has been said is clearly understood, then there is no difficulty in seeing why those who consistently apply Covenant Theology's view of law totally miss the boat whenever they attempt to establish a theocracy with the use of the steel sword. The "eye for eye and tooth for tooth" law of justice stated in Mt. 5:38 and the "turn the other cheek" law of grace given by Christ in verses 39-42 are mutually exclusive principles. Either of the two rules may control the conscience of an individual. However, they both cannot rule in the *same* conscience at the *same* time. The "eye for eye" principle ruled the life and conscience of the Israelite because he was under the Old Covenant or Law of Moses. The "turn the other cheek" principle is to rule the life and conscience of a believer today because he lives under the New Covenant of grace established by Christ.

The Old Covenant "eye for eye" principle cannot possibly be turned into the New Covenant "turn the other cheek" principle and made the basis upon which a judge would settle fights among individuals. How could the law force a man to turn his other cheek if he refused to do so? The moment you use the *power of law to force turning the other cheek* you have violated the very law of "turn the other cheek."

We are glad that the *principle*, and not the letter, of the law found in Mt. 5:38, is the law of our land today. Some Christians are advocating that we should fight to have the letter of the Old Covenant law become the law of our country. They want to get that law enforced by the power of civil government. May God save our country from such people! However, we would also hope that neither ultra liberals nor sincere pacifists will ever be allowed to make Mt. 5:39-42 the law of the land. The crooks will have the law on their side. We rejoice in the principle of grace taught in these verses. However, a judge cannot use the force of law to apply to society the demands that Christ laid on His disciples in these verses.

"Eye for eye and tooth for tooth" is a good and righteous basis for the "law of the land." It was Israel's rule of life under the Old Covenant, but it is *not* the believer's rule of life in the Church under the New Covenant. We have a much higher and more demanding rule stated in the clear objective commandments contained in the Sermon on the Mount and the rest of the New Testament Scriptures.

"If any man shall sue you at law, and take thy coat, let him have thy cloak also" is beyond the power of a law or a magistrate to either demand or enforce. But the power of grace can and does both demand and enable us to keep this very law. In fact, when the situation involves a "brother" and the reputation of the gospel is at stake, we are told to suffer being defrauded for the testimony of the gospel out of obedience to this new law.

Christ tells us to give our adversary *both* our coat and our cloak without even *going to court to seek justice* if the testimony of the gospel is at stake. The true legalist simple cannot either understand or practice this kind of "law."

Law based on strict justice demands that evil be resisted and punished. Grace can suffer injustice for Christ's sake. Some may say we have "tolerated evil" and "despised the law," but our New Lawgiver has so commanded us in this case and we leave our defense to Him. The victory of grace by the power of love is greater than the victory of law by the power of the sword. The Law of Moses would not have allowed Paul to write the following:

> *The very fact that you have law suits among you means you have been completely defeated. Why not rather be wronged? Why not rather be cheated?*
>
> I Cor. 6:7

Why not indeed be wronged without retaliation, if we are truly "under grace" and obeying this new law is pleasing to our Sovereign King?

---

[36]Dr. Robert Morey has an excellent study on this point. It is entitled, "The Relationship between the Old and New Covenants." It is available on cassette tape from *Crowne Publications Inc.,* PO Box 688, Southbridge, Mass., 01550.

Summary

We believe it is impossible to be honest with Christ's contrasts in the Sermon on the Mount and not see that He is making new and higher moral demands than Moses ever made simply because His demands or laws are based on the cross and pure grace. Christ is saying things that were not stated in the law in the Old Testament Scriptures nor can all of the things that He said be "logically deduced" from that covenant or those Scriptures. Some of the truth that Christ taught cannot be known apart from the New Testament Scriptures. And some of these new demands of Christ could not have been made without a change of covenants from law to grace. Covenant Theology cannot see this clear Biblical distinction between law and grace as long as its whole system is based on "one covenant with two administrations."

We continue to insist that Christ is *not contradicting* Moses as if Moses were *wrong*. Christ is showing that grace goes beyond and supersedes covenant law while acknowledging and honoring the validity of that law. Christ is showing a distinct contrast between a rule by law in the conscience based on true justice alone and a rule by grace in a renewed heart based on true grace alone. The two systems of rule simply cannot be in force over the conscience of the same people at the same time even though the same basic moral content may pervade both. We are not talking about a system of "law," meaning *objectives standards*, versus "love," meaning *no objective standards*. We are talking about

81

pure law contrasted with pure grace and true moral laws being
raised to a much higher level and placed on an entirely different
foundation and motive.

We have not taken the words spoken by God on the Mount
of Transfiguration seriously until we see Christ as the new Lawgiver. "This is My beloved Son" is in response to the disciples
lumping Jesus, Moses, and Elijah into one equal group. God not
only tells us that Christ is unique in His person as His only Son,
but He adds, "listen to Him, and Him alone!" The moment we
understand that Christ replaces Moses as well as Elijah, we will
never again try to have Christ, in the Sermon on the mount, saying, "Moses is the final authority on morals and ethics. Listen to
him." We will take the "But I say unto you" contrasts as clear
and sharp contrasts between: (1.) the Old and the New Covenant; (2.) between law and grace; and most importantly (3.) between Christ the new Lawgiver and Moses whom He replaces.

Bibliography for
"But I Say Unto You, . . ."

Bahnsen, Greg L. *Theonomy in Christian Ethics*. Nutley: The Craig Press, 1977

Barclay, William. *Gospel of Matthew*. Edinburgh: The Saint Andrews Press, 1956.

Barnes, Albert. *Notes on the New Testament: Matthew and Mark*. Grand Rapids, Mich.: Baker Book House, 1949.

Boice, James Montgomery. *The Sermon on the Mount: An Exposition. Grand Rapids, Michigan: The Zondervan Corporation, 1972*

Broadus, John A. Commentary on the Gospel of Matthew. Valley Forge, Penn.: The Judson Press.

Brown, David. *The Four Gospels*. London: The Banner of Truth Trust, 1969.

Bruce, F.F. (Frederick Fyvie). *New Testament Development of Old Testament Themes*. Grand Rapids, Mich.: Wm. B. Eerdmans Publishing Company, 1969.

Bunyan, John. *The Whole Works of John Bunyan*. Grand Rapids, Mich: Baker Book House, 1977.

Chambers, Oswald. *Studies in the Sermon on the Mount*. London: Simpkin Marshall, Ltd., n.d.

Chantry, Walter J. *God's Righteous Kingdom*. Edinburgh: The Banner of Truth Trust, 1980.

Clouse, Robert G., editor. *The Meaning of the Millennium: Four Views*. Downers Grove, Ill.: InterVarsity Press, 1977.

Dabney, Robert Lewis. *Lectures in Systematic Theology*. Grand Rapids, Mich.: Baker Book House, 1985.

Gaebelein, Frank Ely, editor, and D.A. Carson. *The Expositor's Bible Commentary: Matthew*. Grand Rapids, Michigan: The Zondervan Corporation, 1984.

Good, Kenneth H. *Are Baptists Reformed?*. Lorain, Ohio: Regular Baptist Heritage Fellowship, 1986.

Hendricksen, William. *New Testament Commentary: Exposition of the Gospel According to Matthew*. Grand Rapids, Mich.: Baker Book House, 1973.

Henry, Matthew. *Matthew Henry's Commentary of the Whole Bible*. Mclean, Virginia: MacDonald Publishing Company, n.d.

Kevan, E.F. *Keep His Commandments: The Place of the Law in the Christian Life*. Tyndale Press, 1964.

Lloyd-Jones, David Martyn. *Studies in the Sermon the Mount*. Grand Rapids, Mich.: Wm. B. Eerdmans Publishing Company, 1971.

McComiskey, Thomas Edward. *The Covenants of Promise*. Grand Rapids, Mich: Baker Book House, 1985.

Morgan, G. Campell. *Studies in the Four Gospels*. Old Tappan, New Jersey: Fleming H. Revell Comapny, n.d.

Mounce, Robert H. *Matthew*. San Francisco: Harper & Row, 1985.

Murray, John. *Collected Writings*. Edinburgh: The Banner of Truth Trust, 1982.

_____ *Principles of Conduct*. Grand Rapids, Mich.: Wm. B. Eerdmans Publishing Company, 1957.

Owen, John. *The Works of John Owen*. Edinburgh: The Banner of Truth Trust, 1965.

Pink, A.W. *An Exposition of the Sermon on the Mount*. Swengle, Pa.: I.C. Herendeen, 1953

Poole, Matthew. *A Commentary on the Holy Bible*. Mclean, Virginia: MacDonald Publishing Company, n.d.

Reisinger, John G. *Abraham's Four Seeds*. Lewisburg, Penn.: Sound of Grace, 1987.

_____ *The Tablets of Stone*. Southbridge, Mass.: Crowne Publications, Inc., 1989.

Ryle, John Charles. *Expository Thoughts on the Gospels: Matthew.* Welwyn, England: Evangelical Press, 1985.

Scofield, Cyrus Ingerson. *Scofield Reference Bible.* New York: Oxford University Press, 1909.

Spurgeon, Charles Haddon. *The Gospel of the Kingdom.* Pasadena, Texas: Pilgrim Publications, 1974.

Tasker, R.V.G. *The Gospel According to Matthew.* Grand Rapids, Mich.: Wm. B. Eerdmans Publishing Company, 1961.

Watson, Thomas. *The Ten Commandments.* Edinburgh: The Banner of Truth Trust, 1965.

Williamson, G.I. *The Westminster Confession of Faith for Study Classes.* Philadelphia: Presbyterian and Reformed Publishing Company, 1964.

Order These Other Informative And Challenging Books

Battle of the Gods, Morey, 316 pgs., $10.95
A comprehensive and unassailable statement of the changelessness, wisdom and sovereignty of God.

Behind the Watchtower Curtain, Reed, $10.95
Written to answer claims made by the Watchtower Organization, expose the false teaching, cultic practices and to lay bare the secrets of the Watchtower.

Tablets of Stone, Reisinger, 96 pgs., $6.95
A study of the nature and function of the Ten Commandments in the history of redemption as they relate to the nation of Israel and the Christian church.

Death And the Afterlife, Morey, 315 pgs., $12.95
The most significant work on the subject of death in a century. It defends the Christian position that man has an immortal soul.

Here Is Your God, Morey, 146 pgs., $9.95
A definitive study of the nature and attributes of God based on Biblical Truths.

Horoscopes And the Christian, Morey, 64 pgs., $2.95
The number one worldwide best seller on astrology from a Christian perspective.

How to Keep Your Faith While In College, Morey, 160 pgs., $10.95
Survival manual for high school and college age students which gives the information they need to be faithful to the Lord while in college.

How to Keep Your Kids Drug Free, Morey, 120 pgs., $4.95

A practical "How to" manual for parents, pastors, teachers, youth groups and schools which gives a solid Biblical basis for saying "No to Drug Abuse."

Introduction to Defending the Faith, Morey, $4.95

A survey of the Christian world view and how it applies to history, art, ethics, psychology and marriage.

Reincarnation and Christianity, Morey, 60 pgs., $2.95

The classic refutation of the arguments used by reincarnations. The first Christian book written against reincarnation.

Sovereignty of God in Providence, Reisinger, 40 pgs. $3.95

A Biblical study of six basic principles that undergrid all of scripture as it relates to human destiny and God's sovereign providence.

The New Atheism And the Erosion of Freedom, Morey, 176 pgs., $8.95

A solid refutation of all the arguments used by atheists, sceptics and free thinkers against the existence of God.

When Is It Right to Fight, Morey, 143 pgs., $7.95

The most thorough refutation ever written of pacifism. It upholds the Christian's right to defend himself, his family, and his country.

Worship Is All of Life, Morey, 113 pgs., $5.95

The only book of its kind. It explores private worship, family, worship, and public worship.

Order Form

Name: _____

Address: _____

City, State, Zip: _____

Prices Are Effective Until March 30, 1990

Book		Qty.	Price	Total
Battle of the Gods	Morey		$10.95	
Behind the Watchtower Curtain	Reed		10.95	
Tablets of Stone	Reisinger		6.95	
Death and the Afterlife	Morey		12.95	
Here Is Your God	Morey		9.95	
Horoscopes and the Christian	Morey		2.95	
How to Keep Your Faith While in College	Morey		10.95	
How to Keep Your Kids Drug Free	Morey		4.95	
Introduction to Defending the Faith	Morey		4.95	
Reincarnation and Christianity	Morey		2.95	
Sovereignty of God in Providence	Reisinger		3.95	
The New Atheism and the Erosion of Freedom	Morey		8.95	
When Is It Right to Fight?	Morey		7.95	
Worship Is All of Life	Morey		5.95	

Subtotal	
Shipping	
MA residents add 5% Sales Tax	
TOTAL	

Shipping & Handling Charges

Order to $10	add $1.00
Order $10.01 to $25	add $2.00
Order $25.01 to $50	add $3.00
Order over $50	add 7%

Please make check payable to:
Crowne Publications, Inc.
P.O. Box 688
Southbridge, MA 01550

"But I Say Unto You, . . . "